Restaurant

DESIGN 3

Restaurant DESIGN3

JUDI RADICE

Architecture & Interior Design Library

An Imprint of

PBC INTERNATIONAL, INC.

Distributor to the book trade in the United States and Canada:

Rizzoli International Publications Inc.
300 Park Avenue South
New York, NY 10010

Distributor to the art trade in the United States and Canada:

PBC International, Inc.
One School Street
Glen Cove, NY 11542
1-800-527-2826
Fax 516-676-2738

Distributor throughout the rest of the world:

Hearst Books International
1350 Avenue of the Americas
New York, NY 10019

Library of Congress Cataloging-in-Publication Data

Restaurant design 3
     p.   cm.
   ISBN 0-86636-189-8
   1. Restaurants--United States--Designs and plans.
  NA7856.R48   1993
  725'.71--dc20   92-41544
                                     CIP

CAVEAT—Information in this text is believed accurate, and will pose no problem for
the student or casual reader. However, the author was often constrained by information
contained in signed release forms, information that could have been in error or not
included at all. Any misinformation (or lack of information) is the result of failure in
these attestations. The author has done whatever is possible to insure accuracy.

Printed in Hong Kong

Typography by
TypeLink, Inc.

10 9 8 7 6 5 4 3 2 1

To my dad,
Nick Radice

Table of contents

Larry Bogdanow

Remember, only a decade ago, watching restaurants become entertainment spots. Their creation moved into the domain of Broadway and Hollywood set designers and the realm of the disco. Theories held that diners were there to see and be seen; to be wowed; noise was atmosphere; "make the place lively!" Shiny hard surfaces and spot(ty) lighting prevailed. Dining rooms grew cavernous and glitzy. In these places I felt overpowered and uncomfortable.

We started getting restaurant commissions during the overblown '80s, and approached them instinctively, in reaction to the trends described above. Designing a dining room in a restaurant was not all that different from doing one in a home. It had to be comfortable, warm and relaxed, but also entertaining. Dividing large spaces into distinct areas or "rooms" seemed to guarantee a comfortable human scale, and a manageable flow of service. Subtlety of material, color, light and texture were also required.

We wanted the patron to enter one of our restaurants and say to themselves "what a wonderful place to eat," not "what does all this fancy finish add to my tab?" The times have changed. Many restaurants began to recognize the value in the lasting impression of comfort rather than a fleeting "big wow."

As the cavernous disco inspired eateries of the last decade began to auction off their crystal chandeliers and exotic marble bars, we find that we are still trying to make our patrons comfortable and relaxed. The value of acoustical insulation, once a point of debate, is now an essential part of every design. If you must raise your voice for your dining partners to hear you, or if you know that music is playing, but can not tell what it is, the level of comfort is diminished. Natural materials also play a large role in creating a relaxed environment; Scotch Guarded cotton upholstery rather than vinyl; wood, ceramic or honed stone floors rather than synthetic carpets and polished marble; faux nothing and nothing too shiny. No polished chrome or lacquered brass. Once you accept these kinds of parameters, you also have to stop and ask: how can these simple materials be used in innovative ways? Though basic natural materials may make people feel relaxed, what would also make them take note?

Savoy, a small Soho restaurant (page 175), was an experimental resolution of that question. The owners are both chefs who specialize in creating innovative dishes from simple natural eclectic ingredients. They asked us to do the same. The walls are clad in untreated blond masonite which is often mistaken for a "custom finish." Domestic cherry wood is used for trim and the plate rail which holds the owners' collection of china and artifacts. The floors are end grain fir block for low maintenance and high resiliency. The ceiling is covered with inexpensive, black acoustical duct lining, concealed behind a vault of bronze window screen. This job was executed by artisans on a limited budget but good design was considered neither an extravagance nor a compromise.

The nineties have brought budget cuts in all endeavors, adding even greater pressure to do something simple, natural and noteworthy. People still want to go out and restaurants are often the first choice for the evening's "entertainment." Restaurant failures have created unique opportunities to reshape their image without incurring great expenses at the back of the house. "Redos" are fast becoming an important area of restaurant design. "Down-scaling" is a dangerous concept because it often consists of a paint job and a few menu entries, but leaves the restaurant's identity compromised. No matter what the budget, a more comprehensive approach should take into consideration the whole attitude, including colors, textures and tastes. Often, the budget constraints, while eliminating excess, can also lead to the most playful and creative solutions.

Photo Credit: Frankie Jane

Shawn E. Hall

As an environmentalist who lives and designs in the big city I spend a great deal of my time pulling together seemingly divergent elements to create comfortable and colorful environments. My design process is quite eclectic and political, definitely originating from within my own personal history.

When asked my view on design in the '90s, the two words that come to mind are challenging and amusing. Reflecting as always the political and social climate of our society, we see the development of a more honest and simple palate. As we strive to find that perfect balance of form and function we see the emergence of a more "American" style — one where food becomes the center of attraction and design the backdrop.

In this period of a "back to the basics" approach, we see a popular and fitting revival of architectural integrity. And as we start to appreciate the source of design from this perspective, we begin to strip away some of the pretentious and overbuilt designs of the '80s.

Today we realize that the overbuilt project is simply going to boast menu prices beyond what the market is seeking. Responsible and sensible design solutions are beginning to play a larger role in the designer's process. These solutions are responsive not only to the client but to the resources of our planet as well.

An increasing number of designers, like myself, are using sophisticated and creative paint techniques to achieve dramatic and unique surfaces. In concert with this custom painting, we are also beginning to see the installation of salvaged materials and found objects. The challenge of using found objects not in their normal context to enhance a design is very amusing. One great architectural piece can inspire an entire design just like a great graphic could set the pace in the '70s. Redefining the look and function of an existing piece can also keep talented local artisans working in our communities.

Not only are found objects less expensive to work with, but they also allow us to reuse resources rather than waste new ones. Found objects can relink us with fond memories which are lacking in our daily lives. We long for history. We aren't a generation of people who inherited our grandparents' furniture — yet we long for that familiarity. We feel safe and connected to things we've seen before.

Simplicity is the trend of the '90s restaurant, where the environment created allows the food style to prevail and human nature to relax. Not only can we save money and resources, but we can reintroduce comfortable and nurturing environments into the restaurant concept. Overall, the restaurant becomes a social gathering place not overwhelmed by design. Subtle elements surround you and give you the choice to discover as your senses respond to both the food and the environment.

Designers are being given back the chance to create design rather than shop for it. We can now use our tools of color, texture and light, and rethink the available resources into a new perspective and a new design.

David Kellen

As little as twenty years ago restaurant design in Los Angeles had as little imagination as most of the food being served. Food was steak and potatoes, coffee shops, red table cloth "Italian" or the "Chinese" out of *Gypsy*, with a sprinkling of stuffed shirt "French." Wine lists were minimal. Beer was domestic. And with so little interest in the art of dining even less went into design. It was a dark age.

First there was a breakthrough with the food. In a seemingly smaller world, people became aware of international foods. Chefs experimented with exotic influences. A renaissance had begun. But restaurant design was a step behind. The first restaurants of this rebirth were mostly realized by the owners or chefs; while being simple and understated, they were also limited in their sophistication and imagination.

In the early '80s some adventurous Los Angeles restaurateurs went to a few avant-garde architects for help. Restaurants like 72 Market Street, Chaya Brassiere and Angeli were some of the first restaurants combining sophisticated cuisine with high-style architecture. As one of the principal designers of City restaurant, the only instructions from the owners were, "knock our socks off." At the time, this type of relationship with restaurateurs allowed me and other designers to explore our own ideas of experiencing architecture. As with the food, the spaces combined the history of craft with free expression. People wanted more and this restaurant renaissance boomed.

There is a new climate as we go into the '90s. With the success of all these new restaurants, people have become more aware. While at one time they were passengers along for the ride, they have now learned to drive. As the Renaissance movement in art was followed by a no less important Baroque period, restaurant design is going through this same process. The Baroque period was more ornate and charged with emotion. The swing in restaurant design is now to a more decorated and romantic look. With the increased popularity of good design, people are more enlightened. With the public and restaurateurs being able to articulate their desires more effectively, designers are no longer operating under the impression that only other designers will understand what they are doing.

I became aware of the new climate when designing the new Kachina Grill in Los Angeles, and the new Rockenwagner. The owners involved in these projects had over the years become very aware of design and how it affected the dining experience. They also had a strong desire to influence how their restaurants were going to look and feel. As the architect, I found that it was not as if I were a lone composer, but rather the conductor. In the past, the hardest part of being a designer was coming up with maybe a single idea. During these projects I found that sometimes it was more difficult to keep all the ideas integrated.

With a new sense of the collective I see the art of the restaurant, like most all art forms in recent times, experiencing a Post-Modern era. In the '90s, designers will create a dialogue with their new enlightened users and the look of new restaurants will be as different and striking as their predecessors in the '80s.

Projects

Blackhawk Grille

Danville, CA

The Blackhawk Grille, a 200-seat restaurant located in a shopping center and across a water course from the Behring Automobile Museum, opened in 1991. It features an eclectic mix of design elements drawing from the automobiles of the 1930s and Mediterranean finishes. A vaulted coffer of corrugated, galvanized material acts as a central spine for the space and is offset with low-voltage "string" light fixtures. Illumination is perhaps the single most important design element and is used in a variety of ways to enhance the overall look and feel of the restaurant.

The bar features a laminated, etched glass top with a hidden fiber optic strip that transmits changing colors of light. Hanging light fixtures with automotive lamps, and brushed aluminum rails complement the 1930s classic automobile which serves as a centerpiece for the main dining room.

A colored concrete floor with stainless steel inlay echoes the coffered ceiling and leads the patron through the bar to a raised dining platform on one side and an outdoor dining area on the other. An open display kitchen and counter is centrally located in the restaurant and accessible to all of the various dining areas. The main dining room has large window views of the outdoor water course and of the dining area and banquet room beyond. Handmade wallpaper contrasts with sconces made from auto hubcaps. Ceramic tile is used as an accent feature throughout, including on a wood burning oven in the open kitchen. Accents of copper, brushed stainless steel and a sculptural mobile light fixture in the main dining room add to the excitement of the space.

Throughout the restaurant a variety of types and styles of furniture are represented, from traditional wicker arm chairs and booth seating, to the latest tubular chrome bar stools. Each linen-covered table is spotlighted, and special groupings of flower arrangements and living plants are emphasized with light.

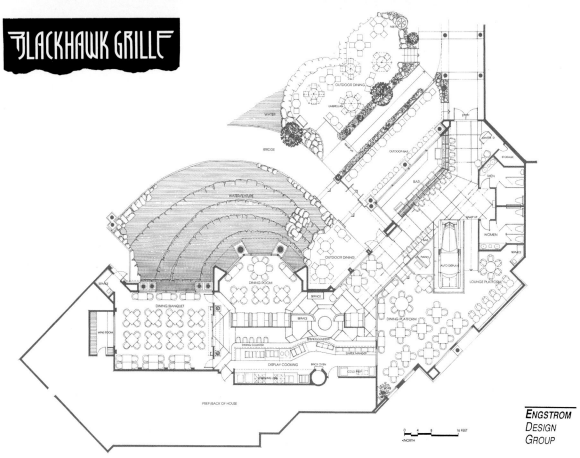

BLACKHAWK GRILLE

ENGSTROM
DESIGN
GROUP

14

Architecture/Interior Design:
Engstrom Design Group/To Design
Project Team:
Eric Engstrom, Barbara Hofling, Jennifer Johanson & Sady S. Hoyashida
Graphic Design:
Tharp Did It!
Photography:
Kelly O'Connor/Eric Engstrom
Type:
Eclectic California
Size:
7,900 square feet
Project Completed:
February, 1991
Budget:
$1,850,000

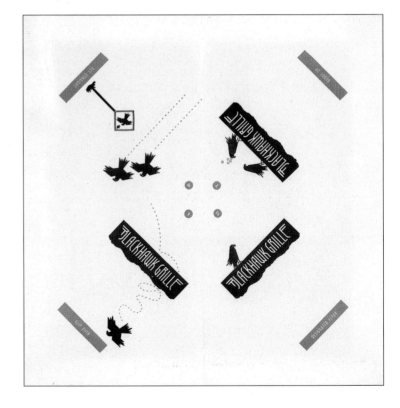

Bloom's Delicatessen

New York, NY

This New York deli-style restaurant updates and enlivens the traditional notion of a deli with high quality materials and contemporary design detailing. It retains all the valued and necessary elements of a deli, the quick service take-out counter, the budget-conscious menu, and the casual and comfortable atmosphere, and serves them up with a twist of whimsy.

Several decorative features contribute to the overall animation of the space. The 50-foot window frontage serves as a transparent display case for colorful, multi-sized jars of pickles and peppers. Hanging salamis and cheeses add a market-like quality to the take-out counter. Photos of New York celebrities welcome customers at the entry vestibule. Mirrored back wall compartments display collectable ceramic and glass cookie and candy jars. A black-and-white checkerboard motif appears in the floor tile and is repeated on the menus and table napkins.

The primary axis for seating layout and circulation is created with a long rectangular cove-lit ceiling coffer. A unique focal point to this is a clock of burnished brass and copper with wavy, colored hands and neon-illuminated numbers. Pendant-style alabaster light fixtures hang in the ceiling coffer creating a rhythm that draws the eye toward the dramatic clock face.

The palette of mostly natural and organic materials creates a feeling of warmth that also complements the serving and eating of food. Terra cotta-colored porcelain floor tile is accented with white marble insets which repeat the tabletop material and add a touch of bistro styling. Partial-height partitions of textured brass and fluted glass are accented with cherry wood. The lighting scheme includes decorative fixtures, such as the pendants, as well as "invisible" fixtures, such as fluorescent cove strips and recessed incandescent accent lights that provide ambient, as well as task-related light.

While practical and functional, the furnishings, materials and design features also provide a richness of visual detail that contributes to the homey, neighborhood feel of this deli.

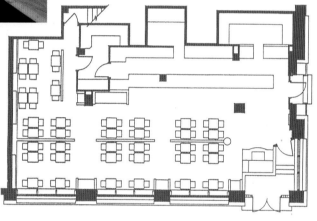

Architecture/Interior Design:
Dorf Associates Interior Design Inc.
Project Team:
Martin E. Dorf, Ivonne Dorf, Lorraine Knapp & Robert McGrath
Graphic Design:
Dorf Associates Interior Design Inc.
Photography:
Maseo Ueda
Type:
Deli
Size:
3,500 square feet
Project Completed:
January, 1992
Budget:
$300,000

Bocce

Minneapolis, MN

Because of Bocce's location across the street from the new Target Center, home of the Minnesota Timberwolves, the design needed to have a sports theme. Since it is such a large space, 8,900 square feet, it also needed to appeal to a broad cross-section of the metropolitan market to be successful. The design challenge was to create an interior fashioned after a contemporary sporting club. Yet, it needed to be stylish to appeal to those with little or no interest in athletics, as well as to big sports fans.

The project required the redevelopment of existing office, retail and public space into a 240-seat bar and restaurant. Programming that space, located in the historic Butler Square building, involved utilizing a former restaurant and a stereo store that had been through several business failures. Part of the problem was a dungeon-like lower level. In order to unify Bocce's various levels, the lower level needed to be opened up and a relationship needed to be developed between all three. To accomplish this and to create a synergistic effect throughout the restaurant, a large section of the middle level was removed to create an atrium. This level serves as Bocce's main entry and its focal point; it leads to a connecting series, including the main staircase, ramps and suspended cat walks that were designed to transport guests throughout the facility. The idea was to create a "see and be seen" atmosphere.

Against the backdrop of the building's exposed beam ceilings and floors of antique brick pavers, a bold palette of black, red, green and mustard yellow was introduced. Emphasis was placed on the integration of the colors through painted surfaces and padded wall panels. The facility is outfitted with contemporary Italian furnishings as well as a custom lighting system. To support the sports orientation, big game trophies such as stuffed zebra, caribou, and wild boar heads, along with leopard printed horse hides and vintage prints depicting a variety of sporting activities, were hung throughout the facility. A pool table and a namesake bocce ball court are available for guest use. The interplay of the various levels and the blend of rich colors and furnishings create a dynamic club-like setting for dining, socializing, and entertaining.

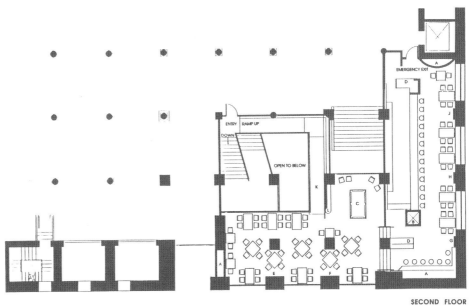

SECOND FLOOR

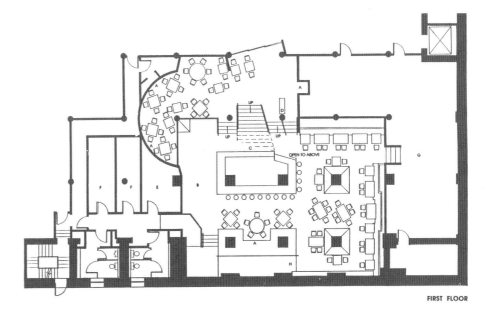

FIRST FLOOR

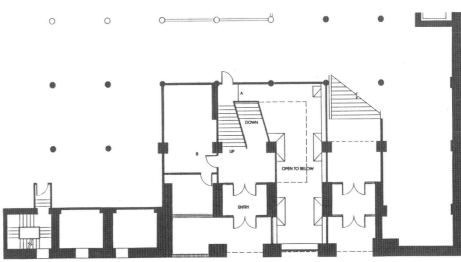

STREET LEVEL ENTRANCE

23

Architecture/Interior Design:
D'Amico + Partners, Inc.
Project Team:
Richard D'Amico & Gerri A. Determan
Graphic Design:
Sara McNerney
Photography:
Tom Berthiaume, Parallel Productions
Type:
Italian Influenced American
Size:
8,900 square feet
Project Completed:
May, 1991
Budget:
$1,200,000

The Border Grill

St. Louis, MO

Like Paul Bunyan and the St. Louis Arch, everything in the Midwest seems to be a little larger than life. The capacious Border Grill is no exception. Here, the problem was that a vast amount of space needed to be personalized and given a more intimate look. The clients wanted to maintain the integrity of the structure, while updating the building and creating an innovative backdrop for the restaurant. Built in 1945, the steel frame structure formerly housed a Mercedes dealership, a bus maintenance facility and an auto glass company. It had been vacant for over two years before the restaurant took it over.

This project demanded an innovative response to the renovation and the designer worked closely with the owners as well as the contractor to solve unforeseen problems that such a unique conversion presented. "It was important to forget the rules," is how the designer sums up the project, "we needed to design a space that challenged the visual senses in order to create an eclectic space that people would enjoy."

Materials used were selected for aesthetic and practical reasons. Color, as well as given forms, relate to the graphics package to create a sense of design unity. At the entrance, diners are greeted by a tortilla making machine. Brightly colored concrete floors were stained and sealed. A giant wall mural of a howling green coyote and a towering 14-foot, green plywood cactus were created by local artists. Furnishings, like the wooden library chairs were kept simple, but were brightly painted.

The custom-designed wall sconces were constructed from steel mesh and copper tubing. The bar lights were made from old stainless steel filters rescued from a former Coca Cola bottling facility. "We were inspired," the designer said, "to use found materials that would not be out of place in such an industrial environment." Most of the materials were chosen for their practicality. A case in point is the ceiling, made from simple aluminum foil-faced fiberglass insulation. Glassblock, corrugated steel and gravel were also used in what amounts to a style the designer terms "neo-industrial techno romantic."

Steve Stradal
Director of Marketing

The Border Grill, Inc.
9119 Olive Boulevard
St. Louis, MO 63132
Fax: 314/647-4414
Phone: 314/997-3700

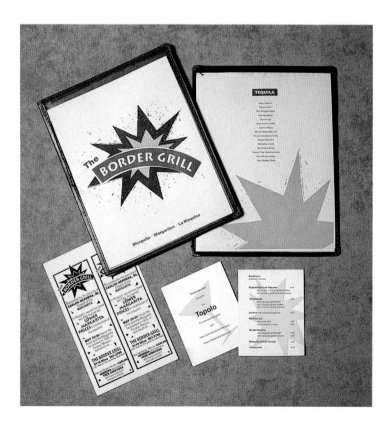

Architecture/Interior Design:
Schwetye, Luchini, Maritz Architects and Ann Sheehan-Lipton Interiors
Graphic Design:
Julie Heller-Rosenfeld, Heller-Rosenfeld Design
Photographer:
David W. Stradal
Type:
Mesquite Grill and Southwestern
Size:
10,000 square feet
Project Completed:
December, 1991

Brain/Wash

San Francisco, CA

*B*rain/Wash is a neo-industrial style cafe and laundromat serving up a blend of high kitsch and low-tech decor, food and state-of-the-art washers and dryers. For those who would rather sit at the bar, there is a wash-dry-fold service available, as well as dry cleaning. The idea was to make fun out of work; it is an ideal place for people to meet, socialize, and still get something accomplished.

The space is divided diagonally by a glass wall between the laundromat with 32 computer-run washers, 24 dryers and a 49-seat cafe. The skewed plan is practical. The diagonal aligns the interior with the city grid and strengthens the corner to emphasize both street and alley. The angled diagonal glass and metal stud wall between food and laundry fulfills an antiquated health code separation requirement. There are concrete floors, beamed ceilings, a juke box with 45s that rock the memory and a moderately priced menu that serves food and beverages that range from beer to espresso.

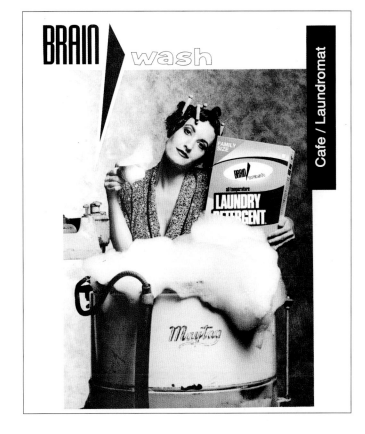

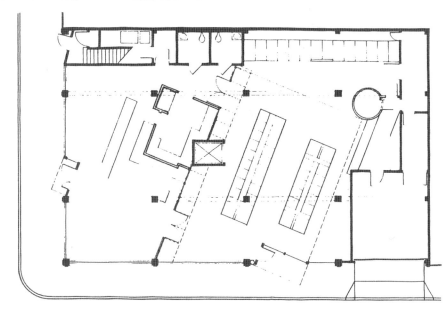

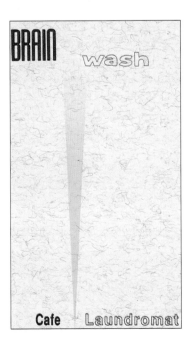

Architecture/Interior Design:
Kotas/Pantaleoni
Project Team:
Kotas/Pantaleoni, Steven Douglas Hornbuckle
Photography:
Jeffrey Meyers Studio
Type:
American Cafe/Laundromat
Size:
3,200 square feet
Project Completed:
December, 1989

Brasserie Bellevue

Chicago, IL

Le Meridien Hotel wanted a traditional restaurant to be located on the ground floor, but needed to incorporate two very different spaces. One was a newly enclosed sidewalk area with limited ceiling heights, while the second area was a sky-lit, four-story atrium space.

The hotel's initial intention was to install a belle epoch style brasserie into a deco style structure. The architects, however, were able to convince the hotel that it would be inappropriate. Instead, they developed a deco style brasserie in the tradition of La Coupole and Le Vaudeville in Paris.

The atrium area was an intimidating and overpowering space. Lit from above by skylights, the uncontrolled natural light cast people's faces with ghostly shadows. To counteract this, a luminous wood grid structure was suspended into the space. This introduced a comfortable wash of light while creating a much more comfortable ceiling height and left a glimpse of what was above. The grids, with their backlit awning, provide a warm glow to the entire room, while creating a beautiful and unusual effect for hotel guests looking down from the elevator or the levels above. The awnings, with velcro attachments, are easily removed to allow for cleaning and relamping. The introduction of the lighting grids from the main dining area into the sidewalk cafe area help to generate a cohesive overall design.

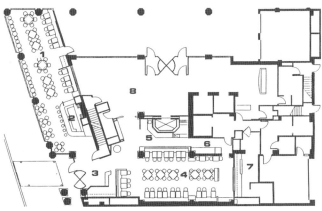

FURNISHING PLAN

1. CAFE DINING
2. BAR
3. ENTRY/HOSTESS
4. MAIN DINING
5. SERVICE STATION
6. BEVERAGE STATION
7. COOKLINE
8. HOTEL LOBBY

Architecture/Interior Design:
Aumiller Youngquist, P.C.
Project Team:
Bill Aumiller, Jerry Milligan, Randy Pruyn & Jeanne Mercer
Photography:
Mark Ballogg, Steinkamp/Ballogg
Type:
French
Size:
3,200 square feet
Project Completed:
September, 1991
Budget:
$450,000

Bridges
Danville, CA

Bridges began as a desire to deepen the mutual understanding between Japan and the United States. What emerged was an idea about "spanning" cultures which spawned a name and a notion about place and time.

Bridges was conceived when businessman Kazuo Sugitani fell in love with Danville, California after his son went there to attend high school. He saw the 175 seat restaurant as a bridge. He believes that, "if you and I try a little harder to understand each other, rather than complaining about the differences, we will probably be able to grow in business and as human beings."

Bridges draws its forms from the memories of the seventeenth century Katsura Palace and the gardens of Kyoto, but is anchored in American architectural tradition. By mixing Japanese garden design concepts with Western forms like the pergola, Bridges builds layers of referential meaning. Blending traditional Japanese styling with the organic forms inherent in the Prairie School, the space becomes reminiscent of Frank Lloyd Wright's Imperial Hotel. Like other early cultural references, the building establishes a dialog between the world outside and the one within. The lofty ceilings and tall windows bring the two worlds together and allow for natural circulation of light and air. The melding of East and West finds its best expression in the intelligent use of natural materials. While they evoke the feeling of the rural areas of Japan and California, the elegant interior employs an inventive palette of elements including limestone, mahogany, fir, granite, brushed steel and glass.

Natural light filters through the windows and into the three distinct dining areas that in turn look inward to one another and outward to carefully arranged views of the outdoor patios and gardens. Overhead, four white kite fixtures float above, washing the dining room in ambient light. Supported by a variety of custom fixtures, nighttime brings a texture of intimacy to the restaurant.

THESE DOORS ARE TO REMAIN UNLOCKED DURING BUSINESS HOURS

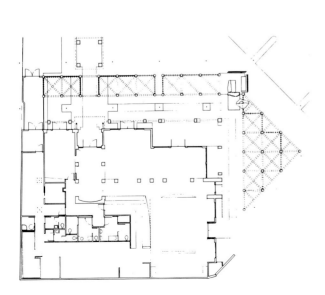

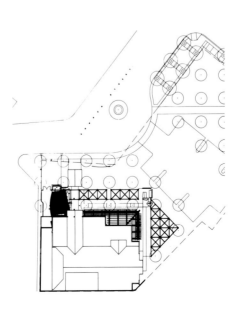

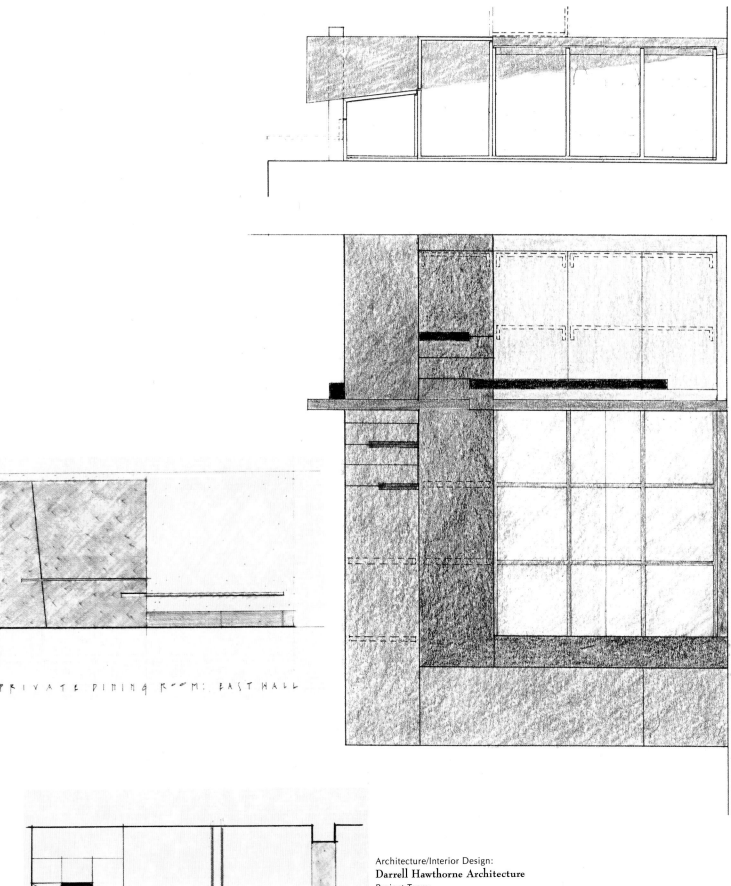

PRIVATE DINING ROOM: EAST WALL

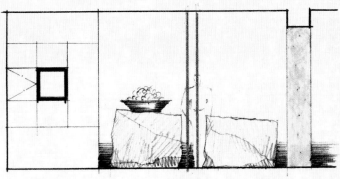

Architecture/Interior Design:
Darrell Hawthorne Architecture
Project Team:
Darrell Hawthorne, Lee Loomis & Peter Van Dine
Graphic Design:
Clive Piercy
Photography:
Ira Nowinski & Darrell Hawthorne
Type:
Californian, Mediterranean and Asian
Size:
4,700 square feet
Project Completed:
January, 1990

Cafe Del Rey

Los Angeles, CA

afe Del Rey was developed from a partially remodeled structure which had been a popular waterfront restaurant in the '70s and '80s. The empty shell, which included already existing electrical and mechanical services, was used as a starting point for the new plan. The design evolved as a contemporary restaurant featuring inexpensive but coordinated and innovative elements and detailing.

By exposing the duct system used for heating and air conditioning and designing custom diffuser deflectors, the large upper spaces were visually enhanced. The high ceiling of the bar and lounge features a steel and perforated aluminum false coffer system which carries the low voltage "trapeze" lighting and gives the area a feeling of intimacy. Green corrugated fiberglass was used to create the illusion of a ceiling in the bar and ends as an awning outside the adjacent entry. The millwork, including the bar, booth surrounds, and low walls was finished in American cherry solid stock and veneers.

A steel and aluminum passage visually divides the dining room into two sections. The views of the harbor were enhanced by large expanses of glass. Reeded glass was used behind booths to separate the pantry and dining areas. The open pantry, finished with a black tile counter, reveals the preparation process of all cold elements, including salads, desserts, and cold plates, to patrons. A prominent feature in this area is a temperature and humidity controlled wine storage display with glass walls. Custom-designed, handmade wallpaper completes the ambiance. Custom-fabricated wall sculptures were created from antique doors and a funky free-form mosaic enhances the fireplace surround.

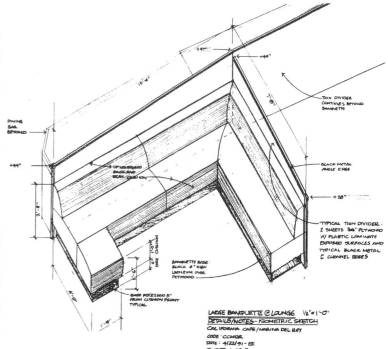

4451 ADMIRALTY WAY · MARINA DEL REY, CA 90292
TELEPHONE 213.823.6395 ● TELEFAX 213.821.3734

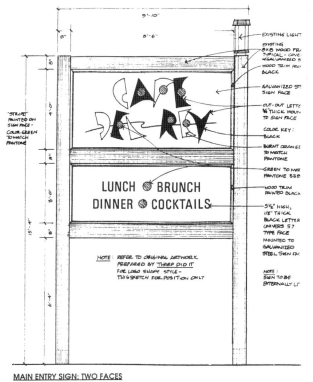

CAFE DEL REY

LUNCH ● BRUNCH
DINNER ● COCKTAILS

NOTE: REFER TO ORIGINAL ARTWORK
PREPARED BY THARP DID IT
FOR LOGO SHAPE STYLE

NOTE:
SIGN TO BE
THIS SKETCH FOR POSITION ONLY · EXTERNALLY LIT

__MAIN ENTRY SIGN: TWO FACES__

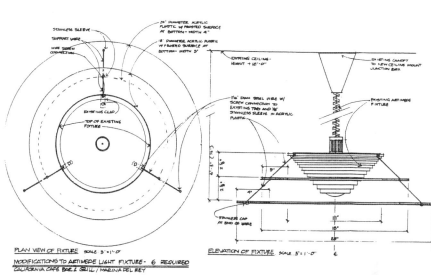

PLAN VIEW OF FIXTURE SCALE 3"=1'-0"

ELEVATION OF FIXTURE SCALE 3"=1'-0"

MODIFICATIONS TO ARTIMEDE LIGHT FIXTURE - 6 REQUIRED
CALIFORNIA CAFE BAR & GRILL / MARINA DEL REY

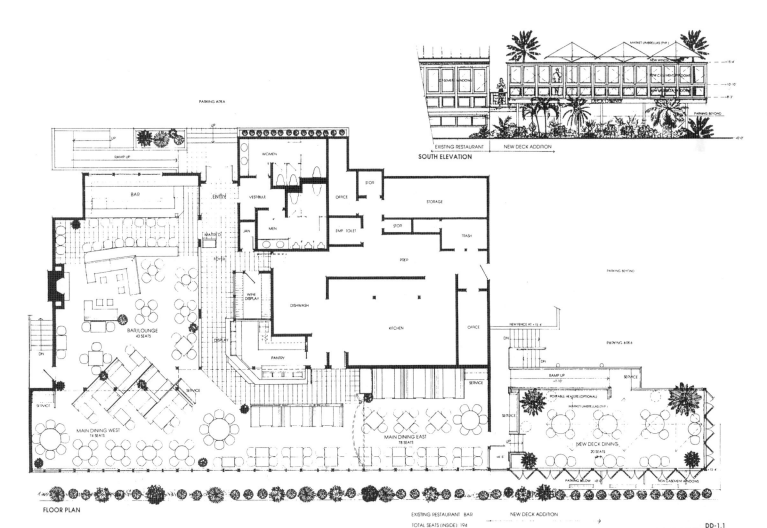

SOUTH ELEVATION

FLOOR PLAN

TOTAL SEATS (INSIDE): 194

EXISTING RESTAURANT BAR   NEW DECK ADDITION

DD-1.1

DECK ADDITION TO
CAFE DEL REY
4451 ADMIRALTY WAY
MARINA DEL REY, CALIFORNIA

SCALE 1/8" = 1'-0"

CCMDR   4/06/92

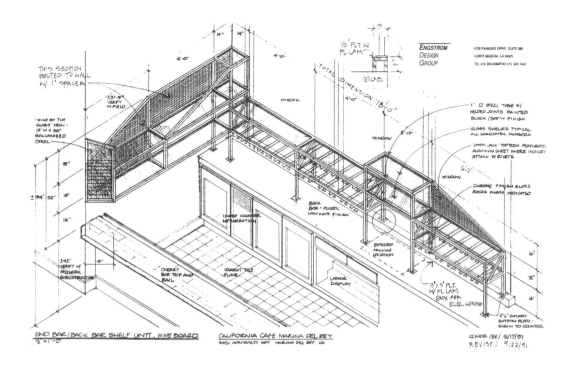

END BAR / BACK BAR SHELF UNIT, WINE BOARD

CALIFORNIA CAFE MARINA DEL REY
4451 ADMIRALTY WAY · MARINA DEL REY, CA

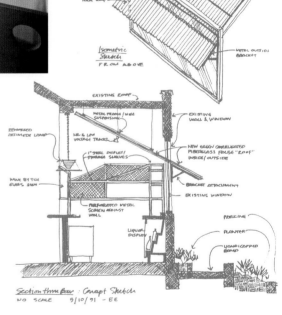

Isometric
Sketch
FROM ABOVE

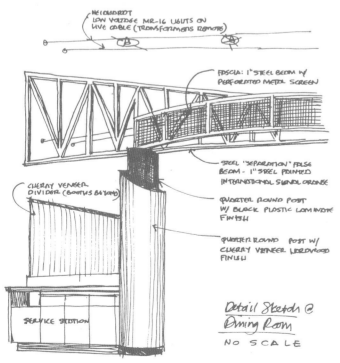

Section thru Bar : Concept Sketch
NO SCALE   5/10/91 - EE

Detail Sketch @
Dining Room
NO SCALE

Architecture/Interior Design:
Engstrom Design Group, Inc.
Project Team:
Eric Engstrom & Barbara Hofling
Graphic Design:
Rick Tharp, Tharp Did It!
Photography:
Robert Berger & Ann Conser, Berger/Conser
Type:
Mediterranean and Asian
Size:
6,500 square feet
Project Completed:
July, 1991
Budget:
$650,000

Cafe Infiniti

St. Louis, MO

The concept behind Cafe Infiniti was to carve a contemporary eatery out of 2,400 square feet of space in a rehabilitated warehouse building in downtown St. Louis. The various elements were designed to mix and coordinate colors, patterns and materials in a novel way. Metals, polyvinyl chloride and bright colors were used throughout to give a unified look to the space. The floor was designed and painted by hand. The heating system was placed near the front windows, on either side of the door, and a raised platform constructed over it. This area, the establishment's most popular, accommodates extra seating while allowing for an overview of the restaurant.

The custom-built bar, in black painted metal facing, is topped in hand-cut black tile with the restaurant's name spelled out in glass block letters. These letters are backlit with fluorescent light in shades of red, green and lavender. Benches, also sheathed in painted metal facing, include a raised curved bench that follows the contour of a structural column, and provides seating for customers waiting for tables.

Halogen fixtures suspended from the ceiling are capped in the evening with lavender gels to create ambient lighting. Philippe Starck's simple metal tables and chairs fit with Cafe Infiniti's look, as do the special metal tabletop vases and candle holders that were designed to coordinate with the overall look.

CONTEMPORARY
INNOVATIVE
CASUAL • ART

LUNCH • DINNER

1305 WASHINGTON
(314) 231-3268

Architecture/Interior Design:
Steve Bowles Designs
Project Team:
Steven Bowles & Clai Green
Graphic Design:
Clai Green
Photography:
Gil Dupry
Type:
Californian and Southwestern
Size:
2,400 square feet
Project Completed:
July, 1991
Budget:
$50,000

Cafe Japengo
San Diego, CA

*U*sing a rich palette of natural materials, the designer wanted to create a restaurant with Asian spirit, but within the context of present day Southern California. Upon entering, diners face a series of partitions that enclose private booths. These partitions are composed of a black metal framework holding bronze mesh panels. As one sees through the layers created by the panels the view becomes increasingly diffused, the way distance is seen through a mist in Chinese landscape painting.

The bar, dominated by an eighteenth century, over-sized Japanese wooden mask, consists of gold leafed panels with the bar top surfaced in polished zinc that undulates like a flowing river. On the opposite side of the booths, a large sushi bar leads into the open kitchen where the solid maple countertop can be sanded regularly, revealing the natural wood surface.

The dining room, surrounded by a trough of black Japanese river rock, faces a bamboo garden. The trough is a reference to water, such as in a dry style Japanese garden, while at the same time allowing enough space between the seating and the walls to protect their fragile finish. Low-voltage lighting fixtures with paper shades were suspended from horizontal cables.

Energy was created by juxtaposing warm, natural materials with clean, contemporary furnishings and lighting elements. Several outstanding works of traditional Japanese art are prominently displayed. The melding of cultures and styles and old with new creates a vital atmosphere, as compelling as it is warm.

Architecture/Interior Design:
Paul Draper & Associates
Design Team:
Paul Draper, Robyn Menter, Elizabeth Smidt and Debbie Debarros Tower
Graphic Design:
David Carter
Photography:
Milroy/McAleer
Type:
Contemporary Asian and Californian
Size:
6,000 square feet
Project Completed:
November, 1989

Cafe La Bohème

Los Angeles, CA

Bohemian is said to be a free spirit who disregards conventional standards of behavior. The designer wanted to express the Bohemian in all of us and capture a feeling of open-mindedness in a new world/old world setting. "I tried to build an illusion," she said, "something universal and very immediate. A place with a lot of visual potential that could be open to all sorts of interpretations." Like Los Angeles itself, Cafe La Bohème is a fabrication, a fantasy from a time and place that never was. The space is multi-faceted, yet manages to be uniquely cohesive. The Hollywood stage-set provides a backdrop within which diners, representing every spectrum, seem comfortable.

Seating in the raised cocktail lounge is provided by a Dali inspired sofa and harlequin-style chairs. A small pool, covered in blue mosaic tiles, separates the lounge area from the dining room. It provides a focal point for a massive sculpture of Siva, the Hindu goddess of destruction and reproduction. The dining room, sunken below the lounge area, can be reached by a ramp in accordance with new standards of accessibility. A massive stone fireplace, reminiscent of those found in medieval castles, is against one wall. The wooden ceiling, twenty-five feet high, is made up of a system of wooden beams and trusses. The dining room booths are covered in red leather and the chairs styled like small thrones. Other materials used include lacey iron work railings, stained glass, copper inlaid concrete floors and red drapes. The lighting is provided by crystal chandeliers and wall sconces fabricated of draped steel mesh.

Architecture/Interior Design:
O'Brien & Associates Design, Inc.
Design Team:
Margaret O'Brien and Fred Rieber
Graphic Design:
Petrula Vrontikis, Vrontikis Design
Photography:
David Glomb
Type:
French and Italian
Size:
4,500 square feet
Project Completed:
November, 1991
Budget:
$400,000

Cafe Toma
San Francisco, CA

The client wanted something fun that would become a local hangout for artists and nightclub patrons who frequent San Francisco's South of Market locale. The architects had to work around the practical requirements: necessities such as a prep kitchen, display cooking, a bar, a take-out counter, and three types of seating. The project was also unique in that it occupied a shoebox-sized space with windows available only on short sides. The designers wanted a slightly Bohemian atmosphere, without the trappings of a room that would look typically "decorated." To accomplish this, they used a device called "interior collage." All the interior elements are thought of as distinct visual components, and their juxtaposition sometimes blends and sometimes clashes. The result is a lively and spirited restaurant. The room was broken into zones to achieve variety within the limited available space without dividing the room with walls. As you enter from the street there are three options available to patrons, the take-out counter, the bar area with stand up tables, and the quieter dining area positioned at the back of the restaurant.

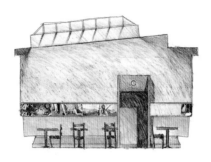

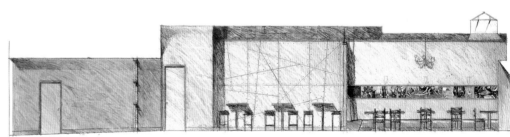

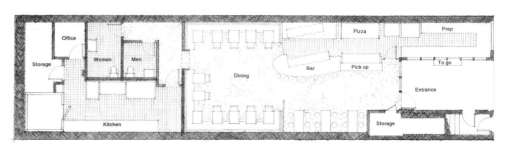

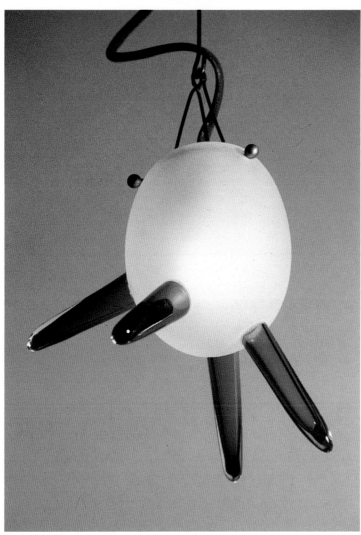

Architecture/Interior Design::
Guthrie Friedlander Architects
Design Team:
Michael Guthrie & Thom Faulders
Graphic Design:
Bruce Yelaska
Photography:
Peter Kerze
Type:
Pizza and Pasta Cafe
Size:
2,500 square feet
Project Completed:
September, 1991
Budget:
$100,000

Caffé Neo

Studio City, CA

This urban coffeehouse was created to be a small and intimate gathering place, a '90s replacement for the neighborhood bar. Of the 504 square feet, only 400 is exposed to the customer. The rather close space along with the visual stimuli encourage patrons to interact with one another. The owner wanted the space to be architecturally distinctive but without hard edge commercial appeal.

Store front windows and doors were relocated to allow the patrons to move easily into the space. The idea was to allow quick pick-up service without disruption to the dining area and to get patrons into a situation where they could quickly and easily interact. The proximity of the counter was natural and defined by simple straightforward masses constructed of plywood. Galvanized bands and a heavy layering of paint were used to give a finished effect without looking too slick or contrived. The dramatic wall sconces were created by a local artist. The simply constructed chairs and stools needed to be economical but had to adhere to a design philosophy that called for natural materials and geometric shapes.

WE PROUDLY INVITE YOU TO COME TO A

PRE-OPENING PARTY

CAFFÉ NEO

AN URBAN COFFEEHOUSE

SATURDAY, SEPTEMBER 28, 1991

AT

11239 VENTURA BOULEVARD
AT THE STUDIO CITY PLACE
(2.5 blocks west of vineland)

DESIGNED BY-GINA MUZINGO
MUZINGO ASSOCIATES

PROPRIETOR-MIKE VLASTAS

Cocktails & Beverages   8-11:30 PM
Provided

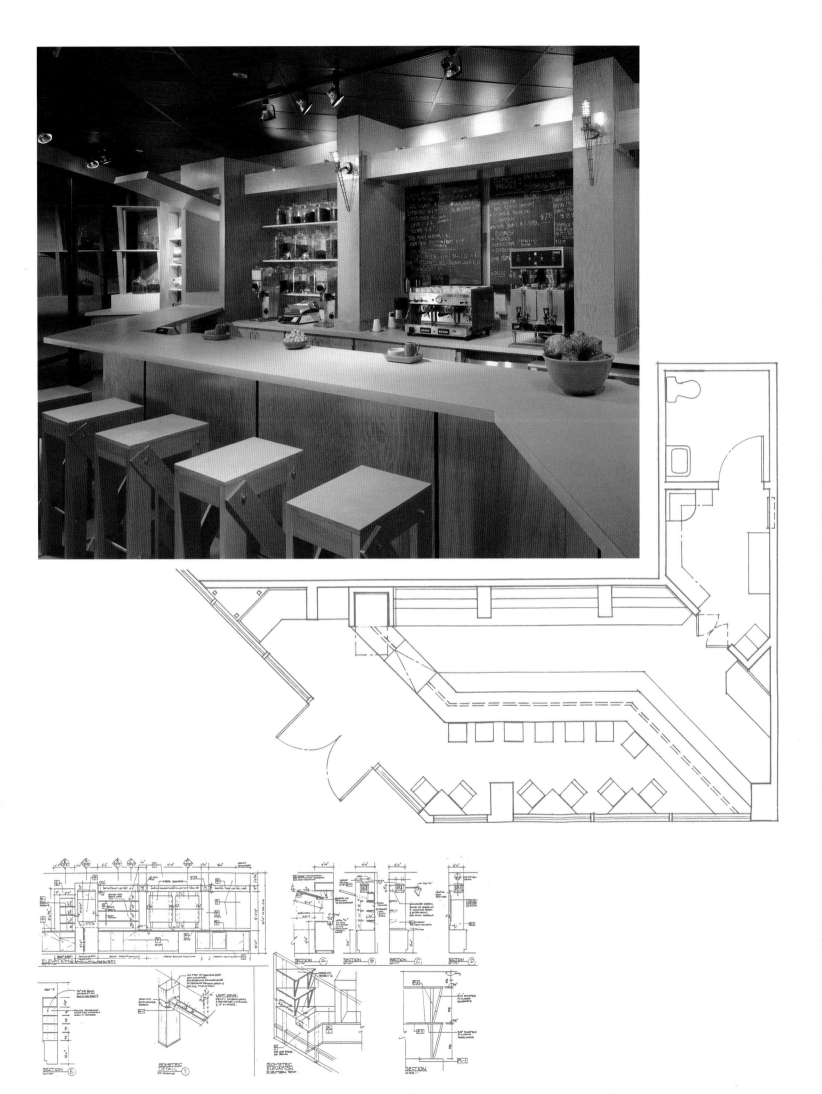

Architecture/Interior Design:
Muzingo Associates
Project Team:
Gina Muzingo, Jonathon Turnbull
Graphic Design:
Christine Wakim
Photography:
Ron Pollard
Type:
Coffeehouse
Size:
504 square feet
Project Completed:
November, 1991
Budget:
$37,800

68

Club Lux
Santa Monica, CA

This sophisticated nightclub makes use of luxurious fabrics and fine detailing. It is sumptuously decked out in bright red and green overstuffed sofas, and chairs arranged into intimate seating areas, giving Club Lux the look of a private club without being "stuffy." Green fringed, red and gold drapes and lush carpets create an atmosphere congenial to conversation. Seating was covered with four different custom-made striped fabrics and a Napoleonic print. The walls were painted with alternating red and green stripes.

The designer, known for his faux marquetry technique, applied it to the circular bar. The curving lower portion was covered with an applied surface material that has the illusion of being three dimensional. He used inlaid plastic on the screens and made them adjustable by incorporating painted shades to cover their window-like openings.

The designer used gold and red silk fabric for the four large light orbs because, "the silk casts a softer, richer glow than glass." Actually wall sconces, these fixtures hang out over the room, suspended from large iron armatures bolted to decorative wall plates. The fixtures are further encircled by silver light rings and punctuated at the bottom by red glass globes. These fun-loving light fixtures allude to the discos of the past.

The stage, two steps above the lounge area, is actually the dance floor. It comes complete with columns, one in each corner, that act as pedestals for four mirrored disco balls. The designer fabricated the railing from brass posts and chains that he wrapped in sheared red velvet. This was created to cordon the stage off from the lounge below without breaking sight lines.

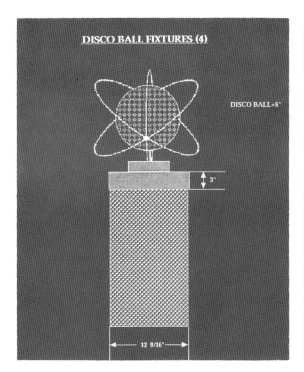

DISCO BALL FIXTURES (4)

DISCO BALL = 8"

3"

12 9/16"

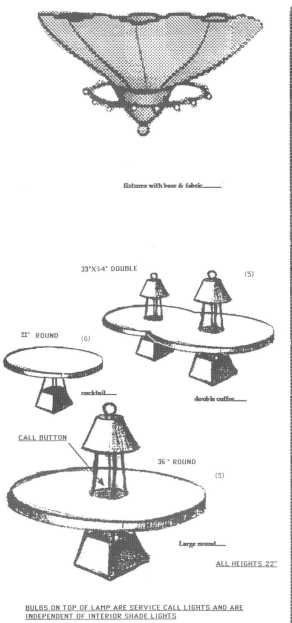

fixtures with base & fabric

33"X54" DOUBLE (5)

22" ROUND (6)

cocktail

double coffee

CALL BUTTON

36" ROUND (5)

Large round

ALL HEIGHTS 22"

BULBS ON TOP OF LAMP ARE SERVICE CALL LIGHTS AND ARE INDEPENDENT OF INTERIOR SHADE LIGHTS

TABLES HAVE WOOD TOPS WITH IRON EDGE AND IRON LAMP/BASE

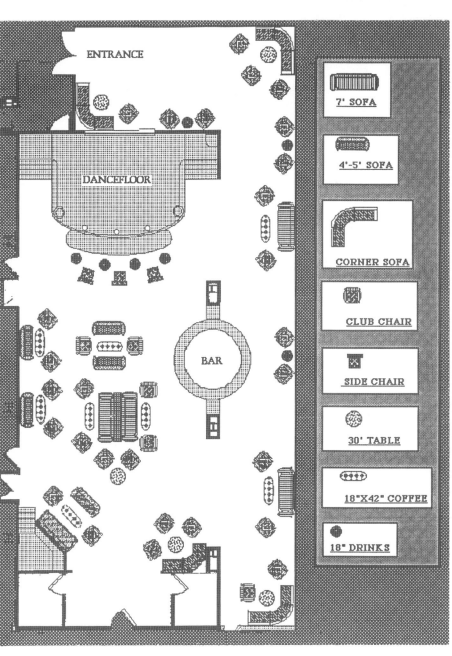

ENTRANCE

DANCEFLOOR

BAR

7' SOFA

4'-5' SOFA

CORNER SOFA

CLUB CHAIR

SIDE CHAIR

30' TABLE

18"X42" COFFEE

18" DRINKS

Architecture/Interior Design:
Ron Meyers Design
Design Team:
Ron Meyers
Graphic Design:
Ron Meyers
Photography:
Tim Street-Porter
Type:
California
Size:
2,500 square feet
Project Completed:
July, 1991
Budget:
$210,000

Crêpe à la Carte

Washington, DC

An irregularly shaped room on the ground floor of an historic 1920s office building, Crêpe à la Carte is a small French style restaurant with indoor seating, a food-to-go counter and a sidewalk cafe. The client wanted, "cheerful yet understated continental elegance," and the designer met this challenge while working under a number of constraints. The building's main fresh air intake and all the main electrical conduits traverse the space. These were concealed using a monumental Doric pilaster that also covers a protruding structural column. In order to take maximum advantage of the ceiling's volume, a huge duct that disrupted the space was concealed with a double curvature lighting cove that smoothly terminates against the existing ceiling.

Approximately 30 pieces of equipment had to be fitted into the work area, including a computerized ordering system, four crepe griddles, a convection oven, a soda fountain and a self-serve refrigerator. The list of equipment was increased during the design process as planning allowed for more capacity than was originally expected. An existing window was transformed into the main entry. Previously, the entrance had been from an adjoining corridor. Direct access from the sidewalk made the space more inviting and accessible, but required approval from several governmental agencies. A back room was incorporated into the design for budgetary reasons and to conceal unsightly components such as dish washing and food preparation.

The crepe preparation counter, a carrara marble ellipse, was placed at the focus of the space. It allows for smooth functional operation behind the counter while allowing patrons to see the crepe making process. A bright and cheerful trompe l' oeil ceiling mural, a scene of bright blue sky and white clouds, is exposed to view by the illusory drawing back of a painted scarlet drape.

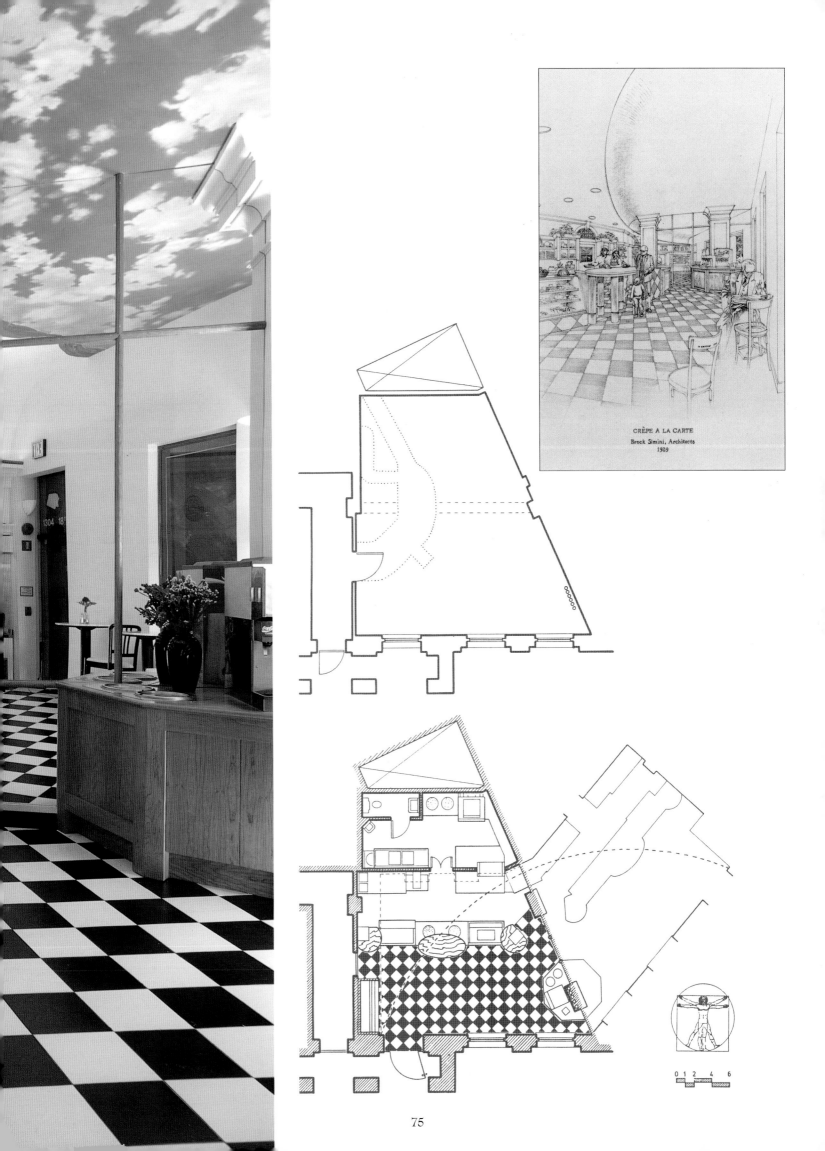

CRÈPE A LA CARTE

Brock Simini, Architects
1989

Architecture/Interior Design:
Brock Simini, Architects
Design Team:
Valerio Simini, William Reynolds & Peter Brock
Photography:
Dennis Kan
Type:
Creperie
Size:
475 square feet
Project Completed:
March, 1990
Budget:
$115,000

Cypress Club
San Francisco, CA

he owner of the Cypress Club has a fondness for the innocent, spirited optimism and community concern that characterized America in the '40s. He has spent a lifetime drawn to the overfed streamlined industrial design of the decade, from the pneumatic cartoon characters, to the films of Frank Capra, and other seamless Hollywood blendings of fantasy and reality. He is a man with a dry, stylized sense of humor reminiscent of Raymond Chandler's "Phil Marlow." So, it is no coincidence that the very name Cypress Club was derived from the fictitious California gambling den in the film *Big Sleep*.

The programming for the design of the Cypress Club began with a visit to San Francisco restaurants designed in the '40s. They all shared several various attributes; bars situated within the dining rooms, high wainscotting with strings of coat hooks along the top rail, leaded glass windows, maroon velvet drapes, wood the color of Anchor Steam beer, copper and bronze metal work, tile floors and cozy peripheral seating. It was these features the designer most wanted to incorporate in order to recreate the era in an updated and exaggerated way.

The entrance to the Cypress Club is puffed up like an old airplane wing and has an animated bronze door handle. The entry area furniture includes a podium inspired by the vacuum cleaner in *Fantasia*. There is also a coat cabinet in the form of an oversized television set with bronze pulls designed to look like cartoon frogs. The mosaic ceramic floor murals and the leaded glass are based on the same pudgy looking animated graphics we associate with the cartoon film *Fantasia* and the '40s in general.

The main room of the Cypress Club has a relaxed symmetry. The main dining area is sunken between two raised seating areas and the bar, allowing patrons easy visual access. Everything in the room is a bit bigger than normal. Overhead there are endomorphic cartoon beams in the shape of cigars. Lighting is provided by parachuting doughnut chandeliers and wall sconces in the shape of fattened plucked chickens. The columns appear to be about ready to pop. Velvet curtains are supported by massive industrial shackles. Flexing bronze "Popeye" brackets support drapery rods and handrails. The coat hooks that were so prominent in restaurants of the '40s now appear to have had too much to eat and take on the form of '40s Bakelite bracelets. A mural inspired by the WPA paintings of Thomas Hart Benton wraps the room in Images of Monterey cypress trees and Napa Valley vineyards. Even the chairs take their cue from the era with curves inspired by the fender of a Hudson.

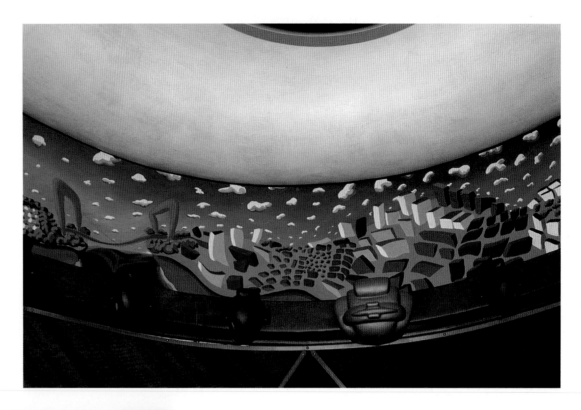

Architecture/Interior Design:
Jordan Mozer & Associates, Ltd.
Design Team:
Jordan Mozer
Graphic Design:
Jordan Mozer
Photography:
Dennis Anderson & Kingmond Young
Type:
American
Size:
8,500 square feet
Project Completed:
December, 1991
Budget:
$1,600,000

Diva Fish Bar & Grill

San Antonio, TX

The building, located in a residential neighborhood of San Antonio, formerly housed a commissary. If there is any doubt as to the kind of food served, a metal sailfish projecting over the building should serve as a tip to passersby. The interior was completely demolished and an addition measuring 8 feet by 40 feet added to one side. The client wanted to utilize the open kitchen concept, but this presented a problem for the designer in such a small, informal restaurant. With its implied coral reef ceiling, ice bins for food display, and a row of TV's, the bar—placed around the open kitchen—became the focal point. Tropical colors were used throughout the restaurant as were elements that would impart a Gulf Coast ambience. The designer used materials such as galvanized sheet metal, painted stucco, and salvaged windows and doors to achieve the look he wanted. Lighting fixtures in the shape of various sea creatures are backlit with white neon. In a bow to reality, the TV monitors are used to display aquarium videos.

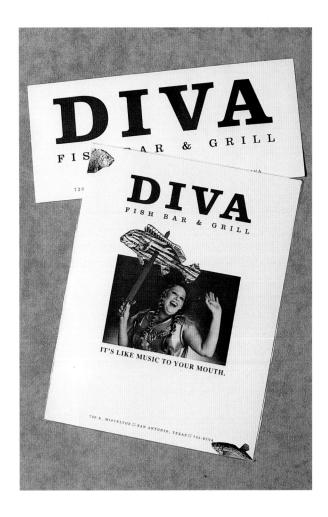

NORTH ELEVATION

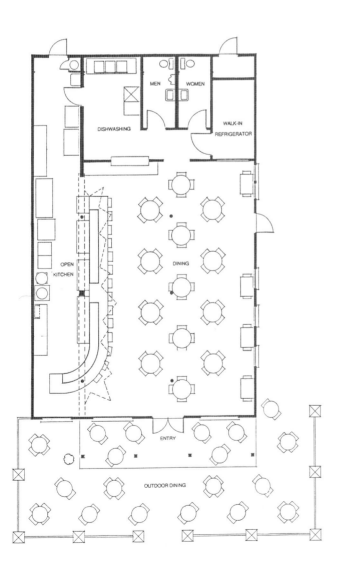

Architecture/Interior Design:
Sprinkle Robey Architects
Design Team:
Davis Sprinkle, Thom Robey & Steve Smisek
Gwynn Griffith
Photography:
Brent Bates
Type:
Seafood
Size:
1,900 square feet
Project Completed:
August, 1991
Budget:
$75,000

Eureka Restaurant

Tokyo, Japan

Located in the Imperial Hotel, Eureka creates the latest in "California dining." The restaurant combines high style and sophistication with a casual atmosphere while adapting to the unique requirements of the Japanese market.

Located on the ground level, the restaurant is near a secondary entrance. It faces the heavily trafficked theater district and the adjacent Ginza shopping area.

The entry was designed with a canted wall, wooden ceilings and marble floors that are carried into the restaurant from the hotel's lobby. Because long lines were expected in the vestibule, a carefully executed space plan was called for. The designer wanted to control the guests' sight lines while still allowing the dining room to have an open feeling. He developed a triangular plan that created a focal point of the main dining area. The dining space is divided and has an eating bar on one side. The non-smoking section, a rare option in Japan, is raised four inches above the rest of the restaurant. It features an abstract mural depicting a vineyard in the Napa Valley to reflect the restaurant's emphasis on California wines. Different finishes, furnishings and architectural details were given to the various areas to help define each space as well as control their lighting and acoustics. Controlled by a computerized dimmer system, the lighting has five different levels to create the desired ambience.

Architecture/Interior Design:
Barry Design Associates
Design Team:
Bob Barry, Masayoshi Ito & Erin Alexander
Graphic Design:
Jacquelyn Barry
Photography:
Ryuzo-Tanabe
Type:
International
Size:
3,000 square feet
Project Completed:
March, 1992
Budget:
$3,100,000

Gordon Biersch Brewery Restaurant

San Francisco, CA

Gordon Biersch is located on three levels of the former Hills Brothers Coffee Building, an historic landmark that has recently been converted to a mixed use commercial and retail development. Sited along the San Francisco Bay, there are unparalleled views of Treasure Island, the Bay Bridge and the hills of the East Bay. While the building has a true presence in the city, it also presented a number of unique problems that the designers had never before encountered. The clear height is only ten feet to the underside of the slab above. Coupled with the fact that the depth was 75 feet and on three levels, some creative solutions were called for. The designers wanted to bring more light into the space to open it up to the view beyond.

The solution was to create carved spaces definable as individual rooms, as well as more "boundless" open expanses. This gives a clear value to the commingling of opposing conditions. Indeed, the project embodies this dialogue between opposites. It is at once raw and elegant, traditional and modern. By maintaining the original rough qualities of the building, the designers inserted richer elements as counterpoints. A mahogany bar is set against the backdrop of the stainless steel brewing area. It is the careful manipulation of the broader palette and the careful placement of materials that makes this space work.

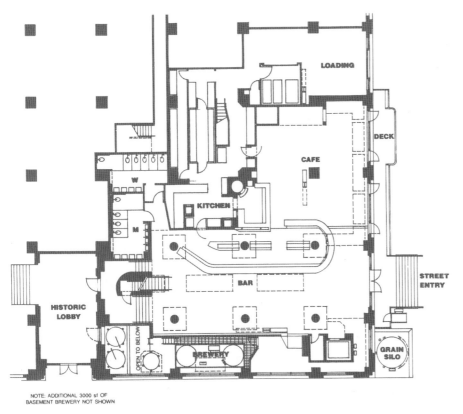

NOTE: ADDITIONAL 3000 sf OF
BASEMENT BREWERY NOT SHOWN

FIRST FLOOR PLAN

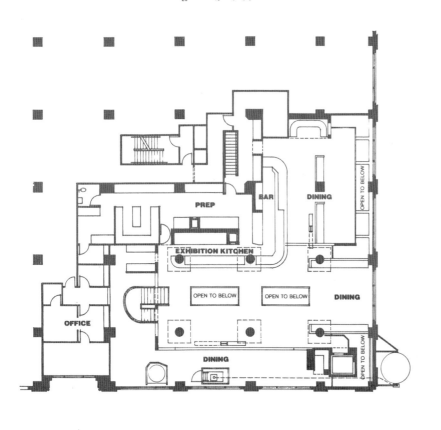

SECOND FLOOR PLAN

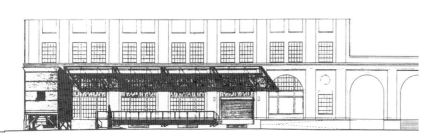

EMBARCADARO ELEVATION

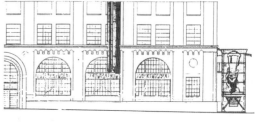

HARRISON STREET ELEVATION

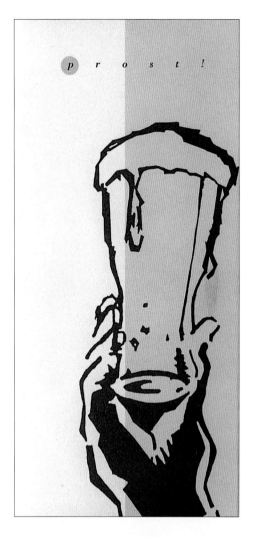

prost!

Gordon Biersch
BREWERY RESTAURANT

THE BEERS

Export A very smooth, medium hopped and full-bodied beer similar to a Pilsner style but less bitter. The beer is brewed using a graduated step infusion mash which holds the mash at various temperature levels.

Märzen The original Oktoberfest beer with a little extra oomph! This beer is brewed using a thicker mash to produce a beer bordering on the bock style. More heavily hopped than our Export and Dark beers, Märzen is balanced perfectly with a higher concentration of malt. The smoothness of this brew should not be correlated with a low level of alcohol and should be enjoyed in moderation.

Dunkles The house specialty and our brewers' choice. A dark malty, yeasty beer prepared by using a decoction mashing process that fully releases the malty flavor of the dark and caramel malts. Requiring specially engineered equipment, the decoction process involves boiling portions of the mash to explode the starch molecules. Gordon Biersch Dunkles is served unfiltered in the old Bavarian tradition of dark beer.

BREWERY RESTAURANTS

2 Harrison Street   640 Emerson St.   33 E. San Fernando St.
San Francisco   **Palo Alto**   **San Jose**
CA 94105   CA 94301   CA 95113
415.243.8246   415.323.7723   408.294.6785

THE BREW HOUSE

Brew House manufacturer: Wachsmann Brautechnik, Ulm Germany.
Pneumatically Controlled and capable of fully automatic operation.
Batch Size: 3,000 liters (790 gallons)

THE BREWING PROCESS

1. Milling of the malt: The kernels are cracked maintaining coarseness of the husks while pulverizing the flour.
2. The ground malt is weighed in the grist hopper.
3. Mashing: Cooking the cracked malt with water for programmed times and specified temperatures.
4. Lautering: Separating the liquid (sweet wort) from the solid matter.
5. Boiling the sweet wort with hops.
6. Whirlpool Separation: The hop particles and protein sediment are allowed to settle prior to cooling.
7. Cooling.
8. Flotation Tank: Yeast is added to the cold hopped wort. After one day, the cold break (large protein particles) is removed by pumping to the fermenter.
9. Primary Fermentation: The cold hopped wort is held at 48° F for 7-9 days. The yeast converts the extract into alcohol and carbon dioxide.
10. Secondary Fermentation: This aging process also referred to as lagering occurs over a period of 5 to 6 weeks. Byproducts of the primary fermentation are gradually broken down. The beer is held under pressure and natural carbonation occurs.
11. Filtration. Any yeast remaining in suspension is removed.
12. Dispensing: The beer is tapped from 1,800 gallon tanks using pneumatic pumps.

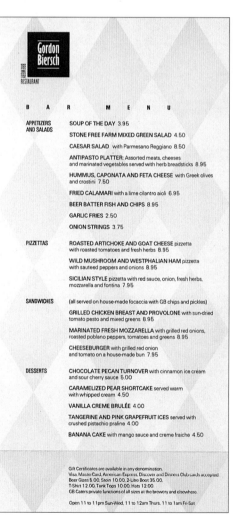

Gordon Biersch
BREWERY RESTAURANT

BAR MENU

APPETIZERS AND SALADS

SOUP OF THE DAY 3.95

STONE FREE FARM MIXED GREEN SALAD 4.50

CAESAR SALAD with Parmesano Reggiano 8.50

ANTIPASTO PLATTER: Assorted meats, cheeses and marinated vegetables served with herb breadsticks 8.95

HUMMUS, CAPONATA AND FETA CHEESE with Greek olives and crostini 7.50

FRIED CALAMARI with a lime cilantro aioli 6.95

BEER BATTER FISH AND CHIPS 8.95

GARLIC FRIES 2.50

ONION STRINGS 3.75

PIZZETTAS

ROASTED ARTICHOKE AND GOAT CHEESE pizzetta with roasted tomatoes and fresh herbs 8.95

WILD MUSHROOM AND WESTPHALIAN HAM pizzetta with sauteed peppers and onions 8.95

SICILIAN STYLE pizzetta with red sauce, onion, fresh herbs, mozzarella and fontina 7.95

SANDWICHES

(all served on house-made focaccia with GB chips and pickles)

GRILLED CHICKEN BREAST AND PROVOLONE with sun-dried tomato pesto and mixed greens 8.95

MARINATED FRESH MOZZARELLA with grilled red onions, roasted poblano peppers, tomatoes and greens 8.95

CHEESEBURGER with grilled red onion and tomato on a house-made bun 7.95

DESSERTS

CHOCOLATE PECAN TURNOVER with cinnamon ice cream and sour cherry sauce 5.00

CARAMELIZED PEAR SHORTCAKE served warm with whipped cream 4.50

VANILLA CREME BRULÉE 4.00

TANGERINE AND PINK GRAPEFRUIT ICES served with crushed pistachio praline 4.00

BANANA CAKE with mango sauce and creme fraiche 4.50

Gift Certificates are available in any denomination.
Visa, MasterCard, American Express, Discover and Diners Club cards accepted.
Beer Glass 5.00, Stein 10.00, 2-Litre Boot 35.00.
T-Shirt 12.00, Tank Tops 10.00, Hats 12.00.
GB Caters private functions of all sizes at the brewery and elsewhere.

Open 11 to 11pm Sun-Wed, 11 to 12am Thurs, 11 to 1am Fri-Sat

Architecture/Interior Design:
Allied Architects and the Interim Office of Architecture
Design Team:
Roddy Creedon, Scott Williams, Bruce Tomb & John Randolph
Graphic Design:
Glenn Randle Design
Photography:
Richard Barnes & Cesar Rubio
Type:
California
Size:
16,000 square feet
Project Completed:
February, 1992
Budget:
$3,200,000

I Cugini
Ristorante

Santa Monica, CA

nspired by timeless Italian design, I Cugini Ristorante
is a feast for all the senses. Designed to reflect traditional
styles in a fast-paced, twentieth century setting, careful attention was paid in blending the past and the present to
appeal to a broad clientele. Uniquely set apart from its contemporary limestone exterior, one enters I Cugini to find all
the classic elements of an age-old family restaurant. Marble,
terrazzo, scrolled iron work, and heavy woven tapestries in
rich tones of cream, black and russet evoke an historical
quality, while contemporary undertones, evident by the various faux finishes resembling stone, hand-textured walls and
granite give the space an updated look. Murals, painted
Manet-style above the wainscotted walls, line the space above
the booths, creating a sense of drama. Delicately painted
sheaves of wheat and flower garlands crown the soffits of the
barrel-vaulted ceiling. The designers introduced parquet
flooring in cherry and hickory to impart a rustic flavor.
Using a combination of low-voltage and custom-designed
iron and alabaster chandeliers, they warmly lit the restaurant
while maximizing daylight. An attached patio allows a spectacular ocean view in a European, bistro-style setting. The
exhibition-style cookline, attached bakery, and wood-burning
pizza oven bring the art of traditional Italian cooking
methods to the forefront and offer a bit of diversion for
interested clientele.

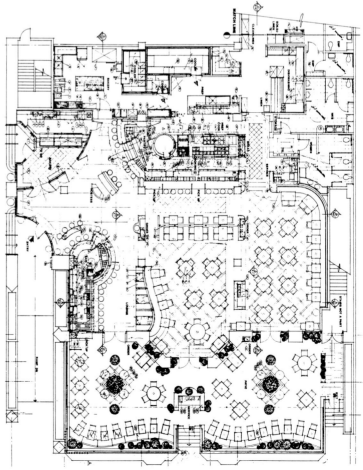

Architecture/Interior Design:
Hatch Design Group
Design Team:
Jeff Hatch, Sam Hatch & Jackie Hanson
Graphic Design:
Marcia Heffering
Photography:
Milroy/McAleer
Type:
Italian
Size:
10,000 square feet
Project Completed:
June, 1990
Budget:
$1,600,000

Kachina Grill

Los Angeles, CA

*N*amed after a Hopi Indian doll, the Kachina Grill is located in the atrium of the Wells Fargo building in downtown Los Angeles. Devoted to serving a varied menu of contemporary American and Southwestern dishes, the design employs strong simple forms to create an abstraction of the Southwestern landscape. The shapes of the high desert plateaus and native building styles are combined with natural stone and colored plaster to recreate the spare terrain common to the region. Sponge-painted walls in muted colors of red, yellow, beige and violet provide the restaurant with a contemporary flair. To reinforce this up-to-date look, multi-colored slate was used as a flooring material as well as treated concrete for the bar tops, and high-tech lighting fixtures. Colorful Native American folk art was used to offset the restaurant's spare contemporary look. Because the existing ceiling space carried pipes and ductwork that could not be moved, space was extended vertically by removal of the ceiling tiles. The remaining grid was painted white and the ductwork above in contrasting colors. With these few lean gestures, an uneventful high rise building space was transformed to a minimalist landscape.

HARALD HERRMANN
General Manager

KACHINA
G R I L L
330 S. HOPE STREET LOS ANGELES, CA. 90071 (213) 625-0956

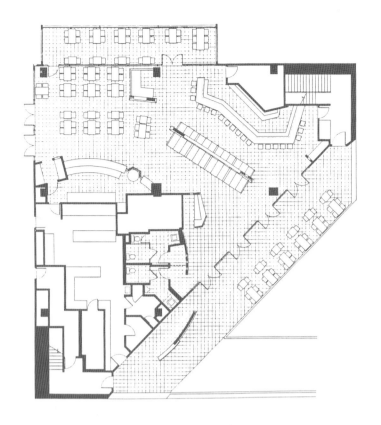

330 Hope Street
Los Angeles, California
in the Wells Fargo Building

(213) 625-0956

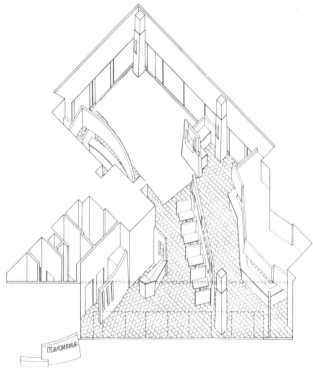

Architecture/Interior Design:
David Kellen Architect
Design Team:
**David Kellen, Taxiarchis Madouras, Richard Corsini, Nana Last &
John diGregorio**
Photography:
Ross Rappaport
Type:
Southwest
Size:
6,000 square feet
Project Completed:
February, 1992
Budget:
$650,000

Le Bar Bat

New York, NY

Quietly and mysteriously located along bustling West 57th Street in New York City, Le Bar Bat is identified by a 14 foot copper bat that crowns the main entrance. Inside, the sacred has given way to the profane at this pan-Asian restaurant and club located in a former church. It is as much a transition from city life as can be had in Manhattan.

The main room is carved out of what was the nave of the church and now is the imaginary "center clearing of the village." The open kitchen and main bar are the anchors at either end of the space. The bar, raised on a platform, was designed to feel like the kind of place one might find in an exotic Asian resort. Angled tree-like columns with oriental inscriptions define and delineate the bar area from the dining space. Swooping above are cobalt blue copper-winged bats that hang between the original gothic trusses. The mezzanine jogs back and forth over the lower level, creating unique vantage points above and establishing an intimate feeling to the seating below.

The decor is purposely tired, almost shabby looking, as though its materials have been used and thrown away only to be used again. Bamboo has been juxtaposed with stained woods, metal and leather. Walls are covered in collages made from antique papers or are rubbed plaster and gold leaf. Even the bar top and ceiling were made to look old and weathered by using decorative painting techniques.

Le Bar Bat is a slightly surreal trek through the wilds of tropical Asia. It is a vacation destination for those looking for a little enchantment; or a port-of-call for anyone wishing to escape from routine.

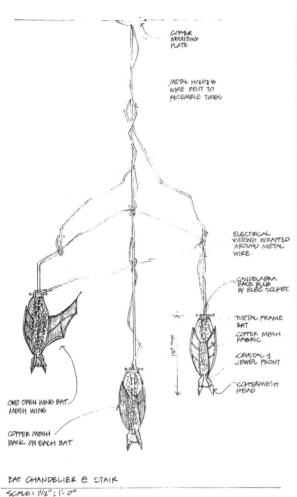

BAT CHANDELIER @ STAIR
SCALE: 1½" : 1'-0"

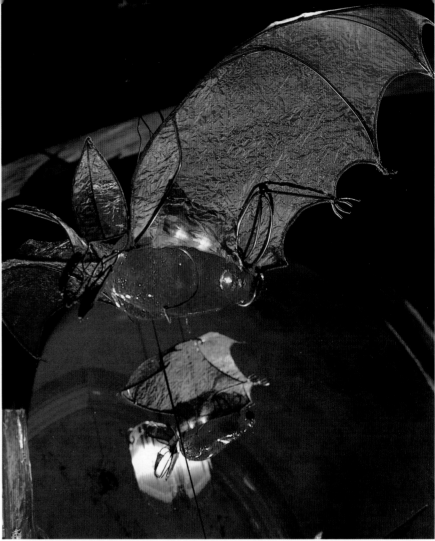

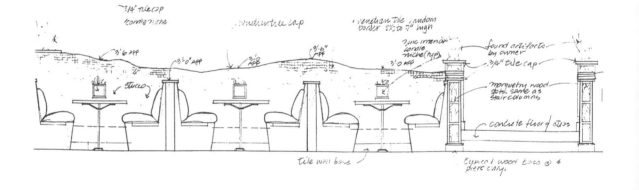

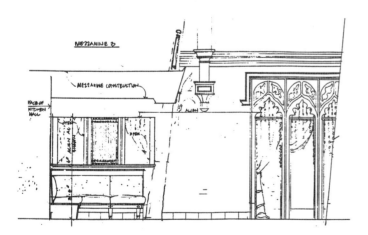

Architecture/Interior Design:
Haverson/Rockwell Architects, P.C.
Design Team:
David Rockwell, Jay Haverson, Carmen Aguilar & James Ahn
Photography:
Paul Warchol
Type:
Vietnamese
Size:
12,000 square feet
Project Completed:
June, 1991
Budget:
$2,000,000

L'Opera
Long Beach, CA

L'Opera is located in the space formerly occupied by the Bank of America in a building constructed in 1900 and now a registered historic landmark. The name refers not to an opera house but rather is the Italian word for masterpiece. The intention was to create "art gallery ambience," a natural tie-in with the meaning behind the restaurant's name.

In order to achieve the look they wanted, the designers did not want to create visual barriers; they deliberately kept the space open. They painted all the walls and ceilings white, and used oak flooring to capture the real feel of an art gallery. They visually separated the cocktail lounge from the dining room by changing the flooring and using slightly contemporary materials. Ground and polished concrete, stained with iron sulfite, was used in place of the hardwood. The iron sulfate gives the normally cold look of concrete a feeling of warmth and the color ties in with the mahogany fixtures.

The building presented some unique design problems because of its age. One challenge was to incorporate a structural brace for seismic stability. This was added to the building during its renovation and instead of trying to hide them, the designers incorporated them into the restaurant's design program. The braces were wrapped in drywall and the space between them fitted with clear glass panels sandblasted with images of Roman columns and pediments.

Another obstacle was trying to comply with new state standards for handicap accessibility. The restaurant, 36 inches above the street, had no provisions for physically disabled people. And, because it is an historical structure, the exterior could not be altered. A lift, installed off an exit corridor, is used to raise wheelchairs from the street to the restaurant level.

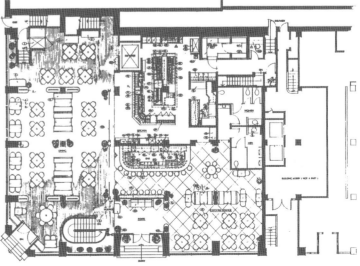

Architecture/Interior Design:
Hatch Design Group
Design Team:
Jeff Hatch and Rick McCormack
Photography:
Don Romero
Type:
Italian
Size:
5,200 square feet
Project Completed:
June, 1989
Budget:
$1,512,000

Marabella's

Bala Cynwyd, PA

This restaurant, located on the ground floor of a "state-of-the-art" office building just outside of Philadelphia, features Italian cuisine as well as local specialties. The space was challenging because of the physical constraints as well as the design requirements. The owners wanted customers to feel comfortable no matter where they were seated. With such a long narrow space this presented some difficulty. The owners currently operate a number of restaurants under the same name and wanted this one to be a prototype for future locations. They also wanted a restaurant that would have broad based appeal, from patrons looking for something informal, to those seeking a more sophisticated and formal eatery.

The space is designed as a series of dining areas representing three evolutionary environments, "water," "earth" and "sky." A fourth area, the bar, is represented by "space." These environments are further used to define the menu selections. Each room has its own distinct personality. The designers credit Miro and Kandinsky, with their primitive, almost child-like styles, as their inspiration. "Our goal was to create a space that acts as a piece of art. Individual visitors are left to interpret and experience the restaurant at their own pace." The result is a dining experience, one that can be enjoyed by young and old alike. The rooms are split by the "path of evolution" that leads from the front entry through each area and finally to the kitchen. Because of the path each area actually ends up being two separate, more intimate dining rooms.

The "water" environment is represented by a ceiling painting resembling a pond with a suspended serpent lighting fixture. "Earth" is symbolized by a series of sculptural, custom-made light fixtures that represent mankind's influence on the planet. The "sky" environment is illustrated by a globe-like sun, a suspended kite fixture complete with a fabric tail and a painted butterfly on the ceiling cove. "Space" is depicted as an illuminated cove decorated with stars and a globe-like planet as well as a crescent moon light fixture. The wine case is an abstract animal that has carved the path through each environment. The animal provides a visual focal point and symbolically supplies music.

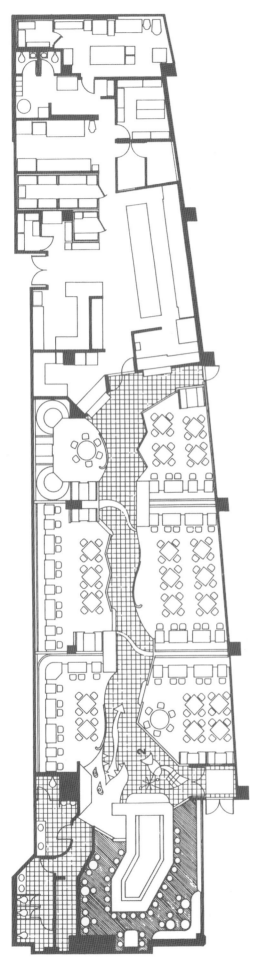

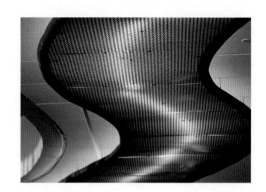

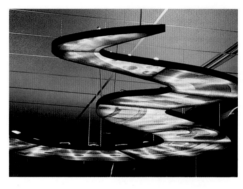

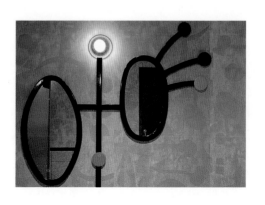

Architecture/Interior Design:
Aumiller Youngquist, P.C.
Design Team:
Keith E. Youngquist, AIA, Greg Howes and Jeanne A. Mercer
Photography:
Charles Callaghan
Type:
Italian
Size:
7,800 square feet
Project Completed:
January, 1992
Budget:
$1,350,000

Mesa Grill

New York, NY

ecause it was the third restaurant to occupy the space, Mesa Grill underwent a radical transformation at the hands of the designer. One senses that the Southwest was a source of both food and design inspiration, but neither is literal in reflecting the region. By trying to go beyond the obvious references to southwestern style such as adobe and natural wood, the design is more about the food and nostalgia of the region than about its geography.

The long, high-ceilinged room, broken up by four tall columns that run the length of the space, presented a challenge to the designers. They painted the columns in an earth-toned red and used a different contrasting color on each of the corinthian capitals. These colors reflect the intensity of southwestern hues, but in shades that duplicate the food. The oak floor was stained black, and the ceiling painted in a contrasting white to create the perfect backdrop for the other brightly painted surfaces. By creating a glass wall at the back of the restaurant, the kitchen was opened up, thus relieving an area of dead space. The artwork, framed singularly or in pairs, was done by the architect and is in the form of over-scaled black and white snapshots. The custom light fixtures are riddled with bullet holes; a reference to highway signs often used for target practice in rural areas of the Southwest. Fifties style cowboy fabric was used on the upholstered banquettes, and large, slow-moving sculptural fans serve as a reference to the desert heat.

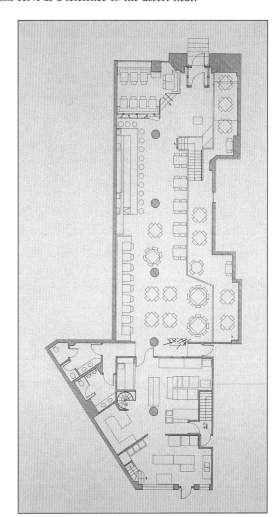

Architectural/Interior Design:
Pentagram Architectural Services, P.C.
Design Team:
James Biber, AIA and Michael Zweck-Bronner
Graphic Design:
Alexander Isley Design
Photography:
Peter Mauss/ESTO
Type:
Southwest American
Size:
4,000 square feet
Project Completed:
January, 1991
Budget:
$150,000

113

Miss Pearl's Jam House

San Francisco, CA

Miss Pearl's Jam House offers the atmosphere of a shady veranda with the charm and timelessness of a Caribbean island. The designer knew she had to create a paradise, a place where one could sit poolside and enjoy a slower pace. She wanted to devise something that would be an escape from the toil and grind of the daily rat race. Since her interests include, "collecting everything and anything and making something out of it," she was inspired by the architectural drama which arises from the limited natural resources available in island cultures. Part of what makes this restaurant so appealing are the rich textures combined with vibrant colors. Vintage metal bicycle and tricycle parts were used to create a railing that would be accessible to the physically challenged and the general public alike. The walls were made to appear sundrenched and as though they had been patched and re-patched through the years. Wainscotting was made with recycled doors, each distinctly different; they were sawed in half and painted to look weather-beaten. The colorful doors are commonplace in and representative of the Caribbean. The furniture appears faded as well, and reveals years of color changes. The custom bar, with an overturned, peeling, flat-bottomed fishing boat used as an awning, was sided in corrugated metal. Beneath the illuminated, glass-topped bar is an ever-changing Caribbean treasure chest, a shadowbox filled with tropical memorabilia. This was meant as a diversion and continual source of entertainment for bar customers.

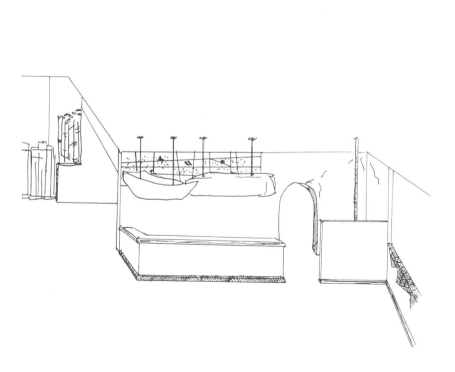

Architecture/Interior Design:
Shawn E. Hall Designs
Design Team:
Shawn E. Hall, Noel Sean Agajan & Jann Eyrich
Graphic Design:
Scofield Designs
Photography:
Michael McSwanson
Type:
Caribbean
Size:
6,000 square feet
Project Completed:
June, 1989
Budget:
$100,000

Nacho Mamma's

Des Moines, IA

Located in the space previously occupied by another, albeit unsuccessful, Mexican restaurant, the owners of Nacho Mamma's were looking for a "hot" visual identity. The designer responded by creating an interior and exterior that are as much a part of the design scheme as the menu system. Because of local sign ordinances, he began by building a scale model of the exterior renovations to give the restaurateurs and city officials a chance to make changes and alterations. The signage was built out of sheet metal and neon. Using the canvas awnings that were already in place, he created graphics which were then painted onto the existing coverings. This proved to be practical as well as cost effective. The results were dramatic. Even the doors at the front entrance were painted in the same dazzling hues as the restaurant's exterior signage. The neon colors and bright jewel tones were then carried into the interior to create a coherent color palette. Included on one wall is a large free-form serpent graphic, painted by the designer. The owners acquired the large jalapeño pepper piñata, constructed by Drake University students, as a barter for restaurant services.

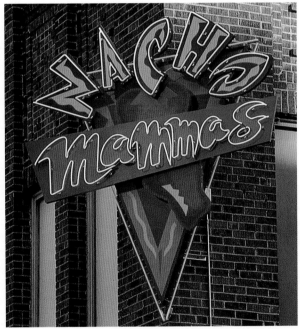

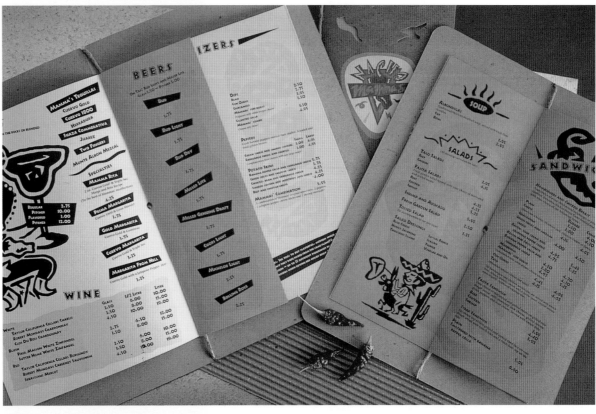

Architecture/Interior Design:
Sayles Graphic Design
Design Team:
John Sayles and Wendy Lyons
Graphic Design:
John Sayles
Photography:
Bill Nellans
Type:
Mexican
Project Completed:
November, 1991

Newsbar
New York, NY

*N*ewsbar is a combination espresso bar and upscale newsstand. Strategically located in New York City's Flatiron District, a rapidly growing design center, it is a modern interpretation of the corner luncheonette. An informal place where one can get an espresso, a sandwich or a pastry, there is also a wide variety of magazines for sale. The design of the restaurant required that every square foot of space be maximized to its utmost efficiency. Designed in a linear monochromatic style, the decor is minimalist. Galvanized metal racks along one wall hold various periodicals ranging from architecture, to art, design and fashion. Flat racks at the bottom hold newspapers. The espresso bar running along one side is an amalgam of concrete, clear metal sidings and translucent fiberglass. The monochromatic interior serves to highlight the glossy cover magazines and contrasts with the early 1900s exterior of the building's facade.

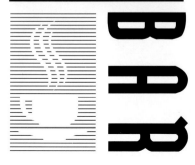

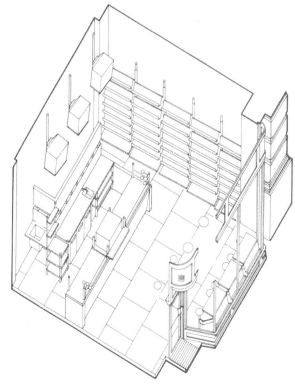

Architecture/Interior Design:
Turett Collaborative Architects
Design Team:
Wayne Turett, Bruce Garmendia, Lester Evan Tour & Noreen Williams
Graphic Design:
Tracy Turner Design
Deanna C. Medina
Photography:
Paul Warchol and Graham Uden
Type:
Espresso Bar and Sandwich Shop
Size:
650 square feet
Project Completed:
December, 1991
Budget:
$153,000

The Original A-1 Border Beanery, Bail Bonds & One Hour Perms

Chicago, IL

The client and designer set out to create a Texas-style beanery somewhere near the border of Tijuana. Together they were looking to recreate the kind of place where the *Texas Tornadoes* would come to jam when they blew into town. While the design was intended to be theatrical, the client wanted the dining room to be comfortable, yet believable. A fictional scenario was created in which the designer imagined the beanery to be owned and operated by a husband and wife team. The imaginary couple, probably Mexican-Americans, were certainly the kind of people who took pride in the food they served. Capturing this kind of lively and friendly neighborhood atmosphere became the restaurant's focus.

Because it is located on the second level of the North Pier Terminal, a former warehouse which was gutted and re-habilitated into an upscale urban mall, the original rough industrial-style construction remained an integral part of the structure. As such, the designer chose to utilize the existing features by imagining the beanery located in an old warehouse setting. With three separate entrances to the restaurant, there was a difficult spatial arrangement that posed some circulation problems for the designer. Two of the entrances opened from the street level and a third from the mall itself. The problem of connecting these arteries to the hostess station, while creating a traffic pattern that would lead patrons to the bar and waiting areas needed to be addressed. A system of "alleyways" was devised; this solution not only solved the traffic problem, but tied into the restaurant's theme as well, while providing arriving guests with an exciting transition.

For the mall entrance, the client wanted a strong breakaway identity from the rest of the shops. A decaying urban facade through which one must pass to enter the beanery was created.

The glass-walled veranda posed another problem that needed to be solved. It would be open in the summer months when additional seating was required for seasonal business geared toward tourism. The owners also wanted to use it as a private function and party room. For these purposes, a more festive atmosphere was called for. A picturesque view of Lake Michigan was a plus, but it needed to be tied into the theme and locale of the beanery. A delicate balance was struck by decorating with cheaply made Mexican party favors and obviously artificial plants and foliage. Again, the building's oversized wooden beams, columns and cement floors were left intact. Carpenters and artists were used to layer the space with two-dimensional Mexican architectural elements, such as cornice moldings and painted faux stone arches that lend a mood of authenticity.

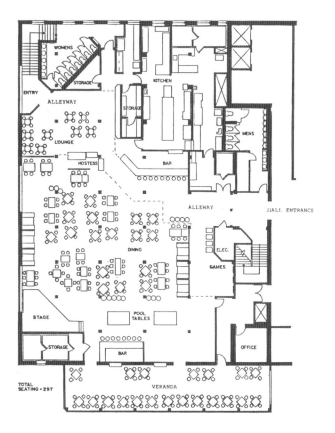

FLOOR PLAN   THE ORIGINAL A-1 BORDER BEANERY

Architecture/Interior Design:
Marve Cooper Design, Aria Group
Architects with Restaurant Interior and Architectural Design
Design Team:
James R. Lencioni A.I.A.
Graphic Design:
Craig Taylor-Yocat Designs
Photography:
Mark Ballogg, Steinkamp/Ballogg
Type:
Tex-Mex
Size:
10,000 square feet
Project Completed:
December, 1990
Budget:
$65,000

Paolo's
San Jose, CA

*P*aolo's, one of San Jose's oldest restaurants, chose a location in the city's downtown which has experienced a commercial and cultural renaissance in recent years. "My goal and greatest challenge," the designer stated, "was to recreate the warmth, charm and flavor of old Tuscany in a contemporary granite and marble high-rise office complex." She was looking to capture Old World flavor and attention to detail in a contemporary setting. A palette that included mustard, eggplant, and olive which is warmly woven through the textured fabrics and carpets, was chosen. "We used huge sprays of freeze dried flowers for color and accent. We juxtaposed the oversized cornice beams and primitively textured walls with loosely wrapped plum, gold and olive taffeta window treatments." These delicate swags scallop across the large expanses of glass, softening the otherwise severe window wall. A neo-classical, European style bar was done in verde patina and a glossy black. For a bit of whimsy, undulating burnished iron hand rails were specially made for the project, as were artistically designed accent tables and a number of lighting sconces and fixtures constructed using traditional materials.

"The most difficult part of the project was that it was not a new restaurant that I was creating," the designer stated. "It was a place that had an established clientele and a long history in the community. I felt I needed to create something new and distinct, but it had to be spectacular. It still had to be the old Paolo's that everyone knew and loved."

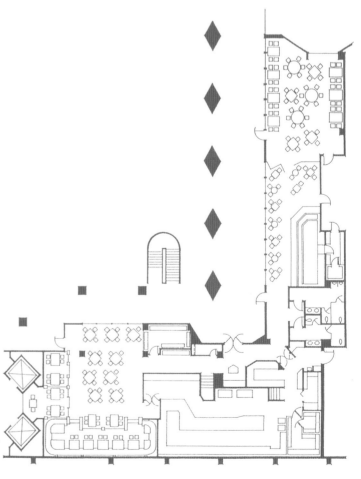

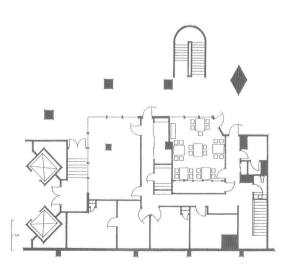

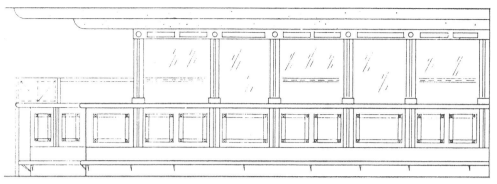

SIDE ELEVATIONS

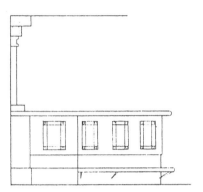

FRONT ELEVATIONS

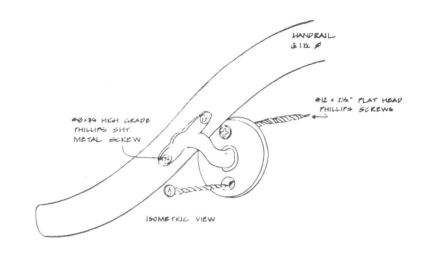

HANDRAIL
ø 1½ Ø

#8 x ¾ HIGH GRADE
PHILLIPS SHT.
METAL SCREW

#12 x 1½" FLAT HEAD
PHILLIPS SCREWS

ISOMETRIC VIEW

BRACKET FOR ATTACHMENT
TO STUDS IN WALL.
BRACKETS ARE SEPARATE
FACILITATE ADJUSTMENT
IN FIELD

SECTION VIEW

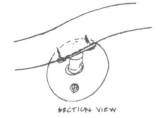

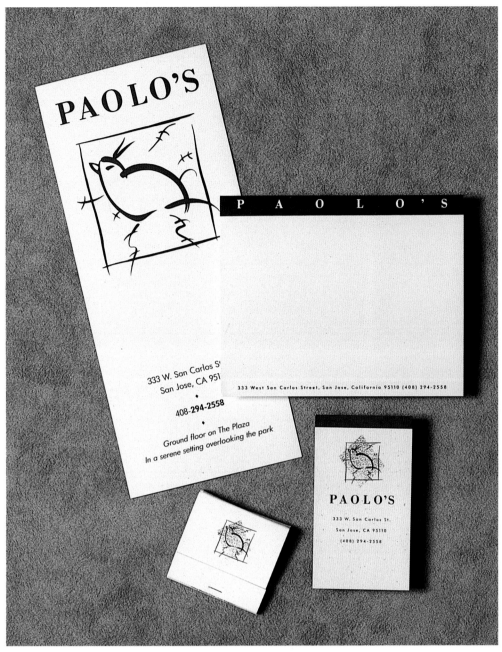

Architecture/Interior Design:
Bethe Cohen Design Associates
Design Team:
Bethe Cohen, Vivian Soliemani, Jennifer Padua, Jim Lyle
Graphic Design:
Jim Ales
Photography:
Beatriz Coll
Type:
Italian
Project Completed:
December, 1992
Size:
8,700 square feet
Budget:
$2,001,000

Piemonte Ovest

Oakland, CA

The building, a one-time residence with California bungalow charm, had previously been converted to a restaurant by former owners. The clients wanted a menu based around foods common to the Mediterranean. They were looking for a space that would have a cheerful and inviting atmosphere and complement the cuisine, but they had a relatively tight budget.

A plan was developed by the designer to incorporate light into the interior and exterior spaces, and open up the kitchen. Walls were given an entirely new treatment of three overlapping layers of colored skim coat, to give a textured, weathered and sophisticated feel. Countertops and tabletops were formed out of concrete playing on the colors and textures of the wall surfaces. Columns as well as arches were utilized to enhance the mood along with natural fabrics used for window treatments and upholstery. The original wood floors were unearthed from beneath a layer of carpeting and refinished. An arrangement was made with a local gallery to provide art work that is changed semi-annually. Outside, the entry stairs were marbleized, and exterior trim was dry brushed and glazed. The deck and patio were then enhanced with new plantings, a fountain, and uplighting.

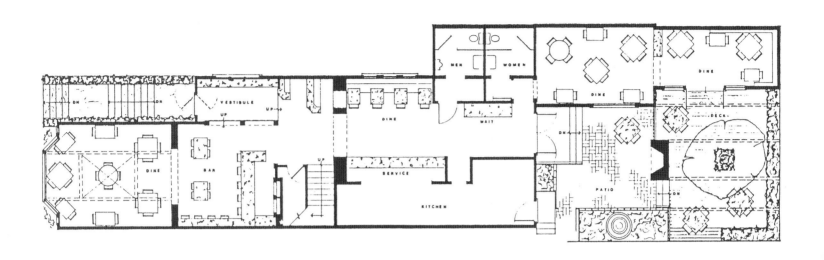

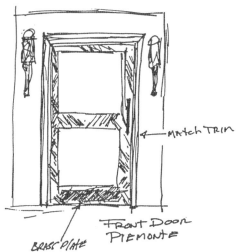

MATCH TRIM

BRASS PLATE

FRONT DOOR
PIEMONTE

PIEMONTE
SWAGGED VALANCE
DETAIL

Gold

ORNAMENTAL ROD

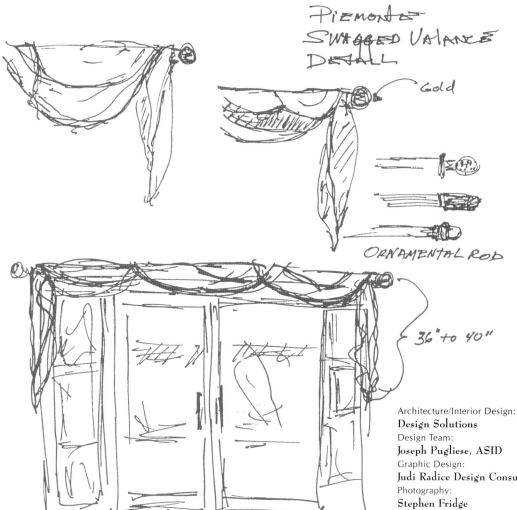

36" to 40"

Match TRIM

Architecture/Interior Design:
Design Solutions
Design Team:
Joseph Pugliese, ASID
Graphic Design:
Judi Radice Design Consultant
Photography:
Stephen Fridge
Type:
Mediterranean
Size:
3,700 square feet
Project Completed:
September, 1991
Budget:
$150,000

Pinuccio Cappuccino and Gelato Bar

Highland Park, IL

Abstracted images that reference historical architectural forms and patterns combined with bold colors help to instill a truly contemporary Italian spirit for this small cafe located in a suburb north of Chicago. The restaurant's main feature is a canted wall painted a mottled blue. The three square niches constructed within this wall are used to display art work. Alternating black and white stripes used on the floors and walls imitate the architectural detailing found in the Renaissance churches of Italy. The ceiling ducts, painted in a brilliant red and yellow, were used to define the space, as was an old Roman vault constructed in a thoroughly modern, corrugated metal. By separating the seating area from the counter, the vault acts to delineate the space without relying on visual obstructions. For a more traditional Italian stand-up bar, the black, friction mounted tables allow for height adjustments.

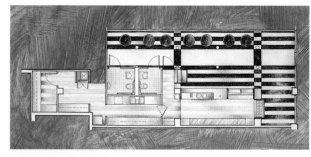

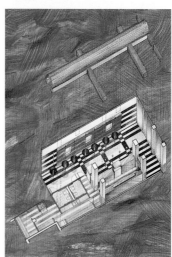

Architecture/Interior Design:
Tainer Associates Ltd.
Design Team:
Dario Tainer, Andrew Groeger, Adrienne Brodin, Peter Juergens, Kurt Williams and Clark Ellithorpe
Photography:
Francois Robert
Type:
Northern Italian
Size:
1,400 square feet
Project Completed:
January, 1990
Budget:
$60,000

Red Sage
Washington, DC

A lot has been said about the American West. It has taken on many mantles, from white man's Eden, to the theme-park of the American soul. At Red Sage all of the unique custom-crafted elements can be attributed to the mythic western experience. The fixturing, textures, colors, organic forms and etched glass were all key elements from the onset of the design process.

The restaurant, spread over 18,000 square feet on two levels and seating 340 people, is broken into smaller "residential-sized" spaces. At street level, it incorporates a walk-in chili bar featuring clouds that flash blue lightening as well as etched glass panels showing western scenes. The tables in this area have tops constructed of concrete and fiberglass and legs fashioned from chromed horseshoes. The booths are covered in shrunken buffalo hide and signed with the owners own logo. The lower level features a series of reserved and private dining rooms enveloped in the rich colors and textures that portray the Great American West. Here the designers created an entire town of western style false front facades. Of note is the two-story stairwell mural featuring four horses that represent earth, wind, fire and water. The dining experience is a showpiece, a Victorian excess of traditional western crafts. The complete range of pieces and installations was designed to illicit a re-enchantment with our own poetic past.

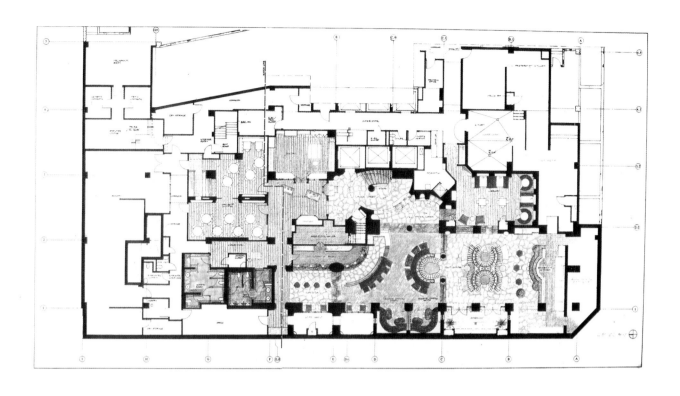

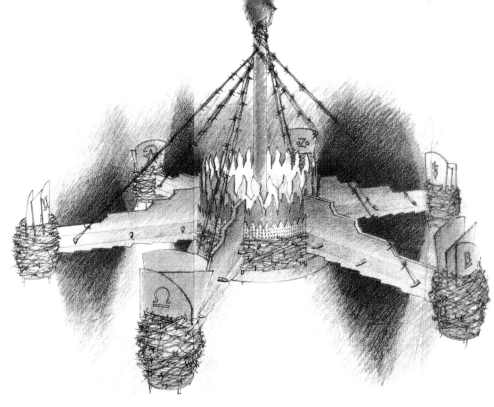

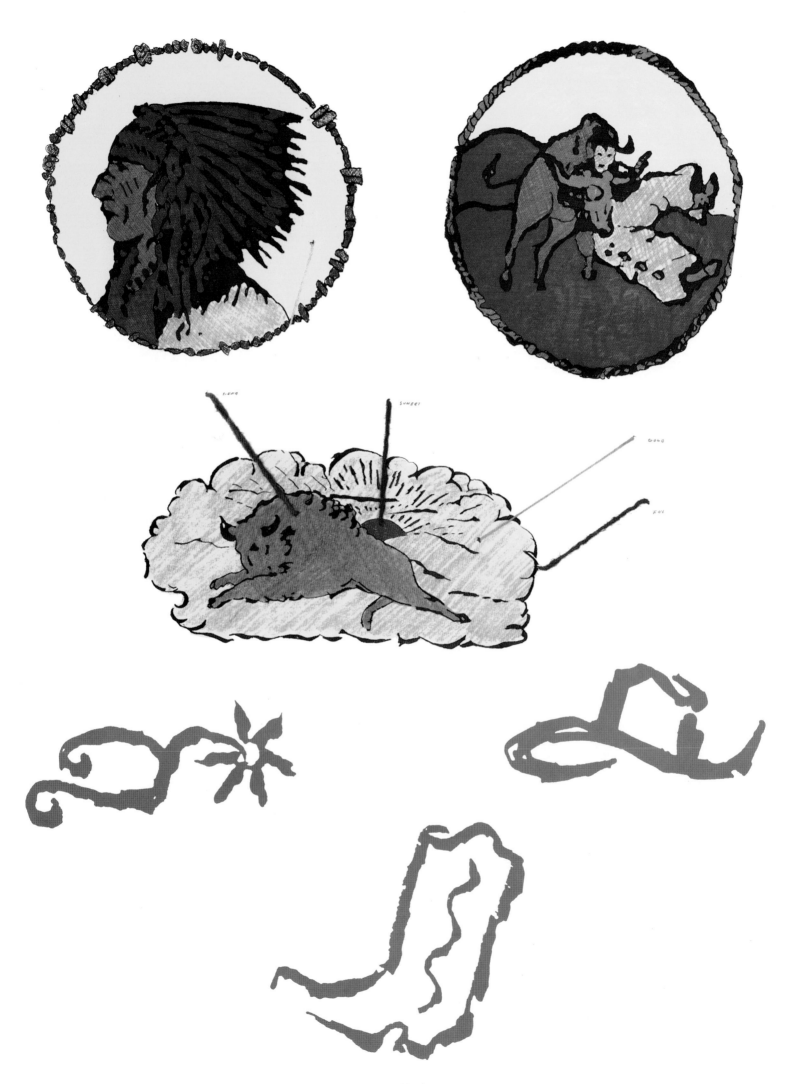

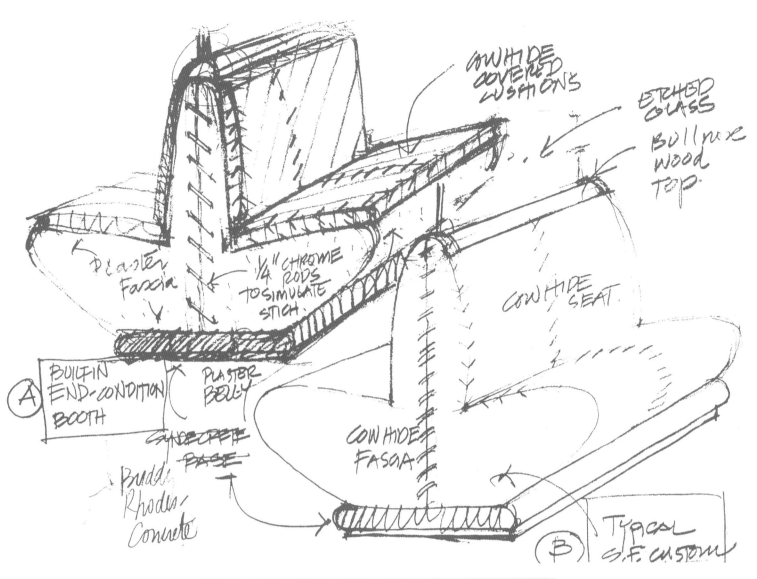

COWHIDE COVERED CUSHIONS

ETCHED GLASS

BULLNOSE WOOD TOP.

PLASTER FASCIA

¼" CHROME RODS TO SIMULATE STITCH.

COWHIDE SEAT

(A) BUILT-IN END-CONDITION BOOTH

PLASTER BELLY

COWHIDE FASCIA

SYNDECRETE BASE

Budd Rhodes Concrete

(B) TYPICAL S.F. CUSTOM

  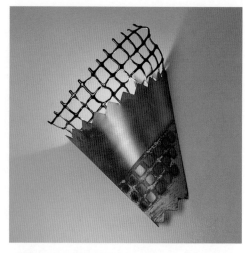

  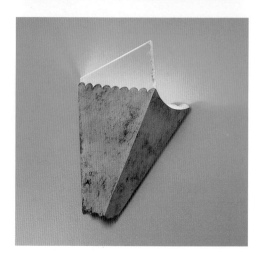

Architecture/Interior Design:
Studio Arquitectura
Design Team:
Stephen Samuelson, Harry Daple and Glynn Gomez
Graphic Design:
Hasten Hunt
Photography:
Ron Solomon
Type:
Modern Western
Size:
18,000 square feet
Project Completed:
February, 1992
Budget:
$5,200,000

Restaurant Bikini

Santa Monica, CA

The program work for Bikini included a study which spanned the specific issues relating to restaurant design as well as defining the client's thoughts and ideas. Looking to capture the theatrical Southern California beach culture of Santa Monica, the client wanted what he termed an "urban riviera" feeling. However, it had to be something that could work within the framework of the restaurant's "modern ethnic cuisine."

Not wanting to create a banal "Beach Boys and palm trees environment," the focus was instead placed on the sensual aspects of the term "bikini." Metaphorical images, such as the sun, sand and surf were incorporated into the design. Architectural elements were organized around "urban" juxtapositions of form and materials which lent function, purpose and play to the space. The designer's intent was to create a dense but subtle layering of refined materials, that play against the space's interior structure of rough concrete.

The form and curve of a "wave" and its cresting motion were used as the foundation on which a compositional layering of architectural elements could be built. Additionally, the lines of a female torso were abstractly interpreted and interspersed with other formal components of function and circulation. The object was to give every patron a view, and to keep the space as simple and clean as possible, keeping the emphasis always on the food.

It was important to impart a sense of glamour, seduction and restraint to the colors, materials and textures throughout. An understated drama of these relationships was primarily played out in deep pigmented, stained birch colored "cherry mahogany," "citrus lime," "celery" and "saffron." The boldness of these wood forms was accented by oxidized and hammered steel, rich mixes of various kinds of terrazzo and cobalt blue glass. The banquettes are covered in plush cut velvets in bold colors with a more durable rafia-woven textile used for the seat cushions. The space is further enhanced by the use of custom designed lighting, furnishings and the "Bikini Chair."

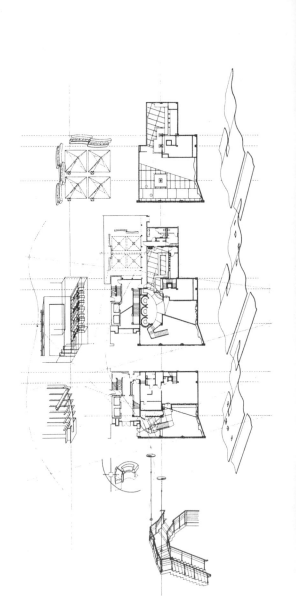

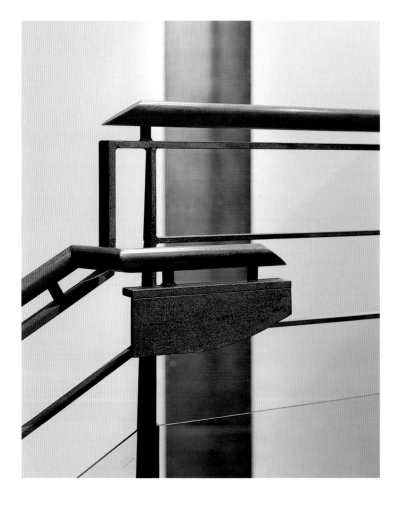

Architecture/Interior Design:
Brantner Design Associates
Project Team:
Cheryl Brantner
Photography:
Douglas Hill
Type:
Modern Ethnic
Project Completed:
November, 1991

161

Rikki Rikki

Kirkland, WA

*R*ikki means *power* in Japanese. Double it and you get *really powerful*. The client, a young Japanese restaurateur, wanted his first restaurant to be upscale, fun and easily accessible to patrons living in the surrounding community. Other client requests included an open kitchen with an adjoining sushi bar, tatami rooms and open seating. The site is a 3,000 square-foot storefront location in a large urban shopping center.

The design concept was for an open plan utilizing the sushi display island as a focal point as well as a divider between the various dining spaces. Tatami rooms with movable partitions between them were located at the end of the space because they had no need for windows and offered privacy.

Materials and colors were selected to give a contemporary, stylized interpretation of traditional Japanese elements and to emphasize contrasting textures and finishes. The black-and-white terrazzo floor with white rocks represents a path. The sushi counter's rough edge and the rounded columns between the tatami rooms are symbolic of nature. The corrugated plastic used as shoji screens, and pitch metal corrugated roof over the sushi counter and in tatami rooms is an expression of materials and forms found in contemporary Japanese architecture.

The focal point of the restaurant centers on the use of *manga*, a comic book style illustration that is popular in Japan.

Manga was chosen to provide both an unusual graphic solution for wall decor and as a recognizable and entertaining element for clientele. Three color schemes were interwoven with the comic strip characters; a yellow background on the exterior walls, periwinkle blue for the core walls and a bright orange/yellow in the tatami rooms.

Custom-designed lighting is both functional and decorative. The forms are symbolic of shapes found in Japanese culture. Low-voltage lighting is used as an accent and provides variations in intensity.

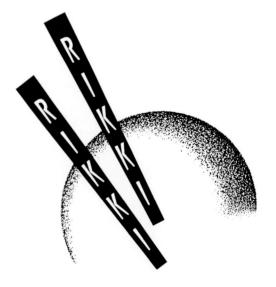

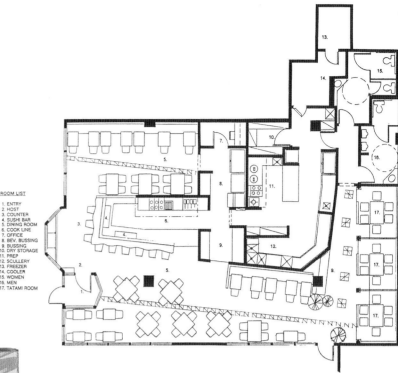

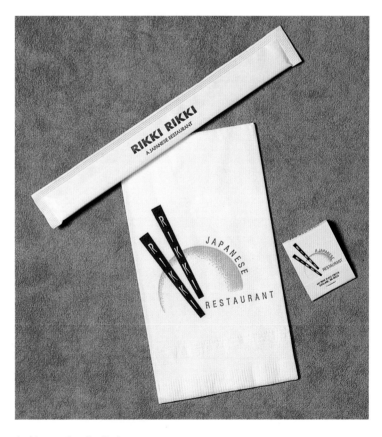

Architecture/Interior Design:
Mesher Shing & Associates
Design Team:
Bob Mesher, Joe Shing and Susan Martinson
Graphic Design:
Hornall Anderson Design
Photography:
Dick Busher
Type:
Japanese
Size:
3,000 square feet
Project Completed:
January, 1991
Budget:
$800,000

Rio Rio Cantina and Fiesta Room Annex

San Antonio, TX

This restaurant and cantina is located in the historic H. Schultz Building on the Paseo del Rio in Downtown San Antonio. The space formerly housed a restaurant so the architects needed to make only minor alterations to the kitchen. The remaining public areas were completely demolished and rebuilt. With an entrance on the River Walk as well as the street level side, each approach needed to respond to the differing urban context and called for a distinctive strategy.

An attempt was made to create a place that had its own sense of history, yet still made reference to the present. Elements in the design suggest the kind of ambience tourists expect to find in San Antonio and Mexico. Colors, textures, furniture, and certain architectural elements were taken from Latin American and South Texas design motifs, but were arranged together in unusual juxtapositions. The designers' intention was to suggest a Mexican border town cantina of the not-so-distant past.

The Fiesta Room, adjacent to the original Rio Rio, is a continuation of the same design ideology but with a different perspective. Whereas the original project dealt with primary colors, the annex uses secondary colors and a more romantic mood. All wrought iron pieces, the chandeliers, and the broken tile tables were devised by the designer. *Mayan Figures*, a metal cutout, was designed by Guy Hundere.

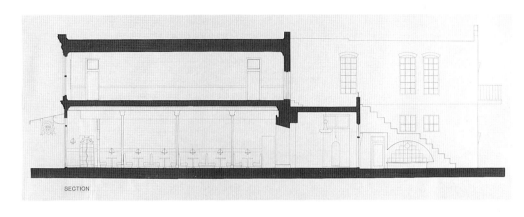

SECTION

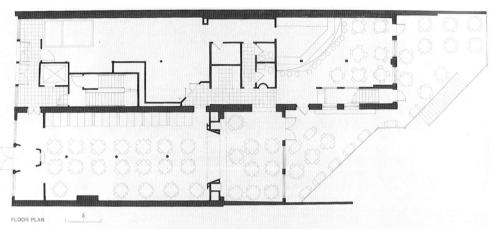

FLOOR PLAN   5

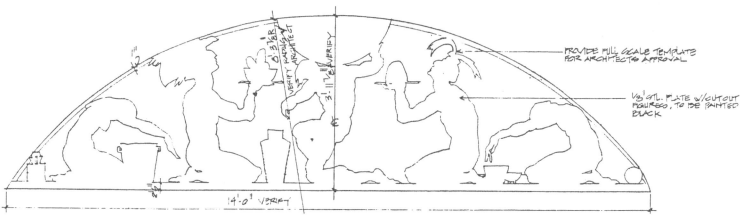

FRONT   BACK

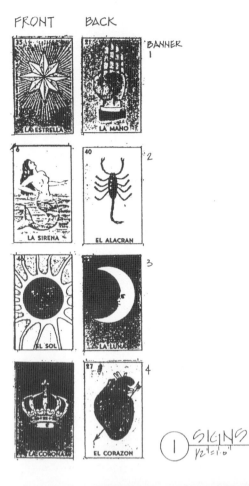

BANNER
1

35 LA ESTRELLA   2 LA MANO

6 LA SIRENA   40 EL ALACRAN   2

EL SOL   LA LUNA   3

LA CORONA   27 EL CORAZON   4

① SIGNS
½" = 1'-0"

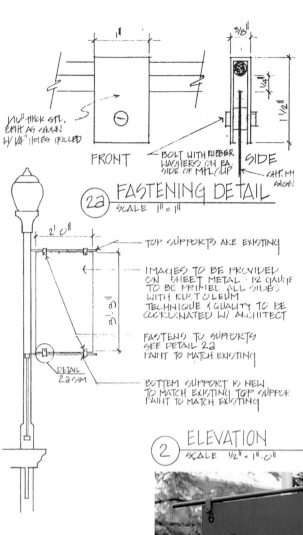

¼" THICK STL.
BENT AS SHOWN
W/ ¼" HOLES DRILLED

FRONT   SIDE

BOLT WITH RUBBER
WASHERS ON EA.
SIDE OF MTL CLIP

SHT. MTL
SIGN

②ⓐ FASTENING DETAIL
SCALE 1" = 1"

TOP SUPPORTS ARE EXISTING

IMAGES TO BE PROVIDED
ON SHEET METAL · 12 GAUGE
TO BE PRIMED ALL SIDES
WITH RUSTOLEUM
TECHNIQUE & QUALITY TO BE
COORDINATED W/ ARCHITECT

FASTENS TO SUPPORTS
SEE DETAIL 2a
PAINT TO MATCH EXISTING

DETAIL
2a SIM

BOTTOM SUPPORT IS NEW
TO MATCH EXISTING TOP SUPPORT
PAINT TO MATCH EXISTING

② ELEVATION
SCALE ½" = 1'-0"

Architecture/Interior Design:
Sprinkle Robey Architects
Design Team:
Davis Sprinkle, Thom Robey and Carlos Garcia
Graphic Design:
Koy Design
Photography:
John Dyer and Brent Bates
Type:
Mexican
Size:
4,100 & 3,000 square feet
Project Completed:
1990–92
Budget:
$400,000

Savoy
New York, NY

The designers of Savoy sought to provide a warm quiet atmosphere that would support the creative cuisine rather than compete with it. They found that severe budget limitations can often lead to the richest solutions. In a bow to whimsy, the assembled finishes celebrate their pedestrian origins. For the ceiling, a curved framework of cherrywood was sheathed with layers of bronze window screen and backlit to create a moire effect. The simple blonde Masonite wall panels were also framed in cherry and give the room an almost Arts and Crafts look. A strong contrast is created by the rough texture of the exposed brick fireplace and the end grain block flooring usually associated with factories. Exterior lighting was made using chef's funnels to illuminate the sign above. At the entry, lighting fixtures were created by utilizing sugar scoops and masonry tieback stars.

SAVOY

70 PRINCE STREET NYC   219-8570

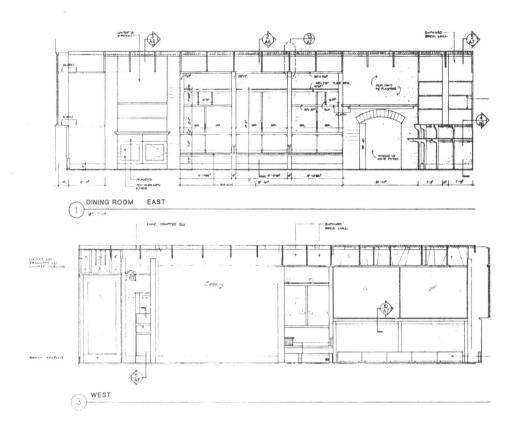

① DINING ROOM   EAST

③ WEST

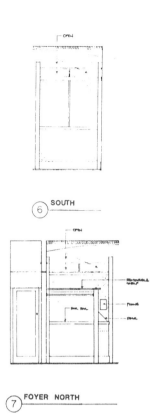

⑥ SOUTH

⑦ FOYER NORTH

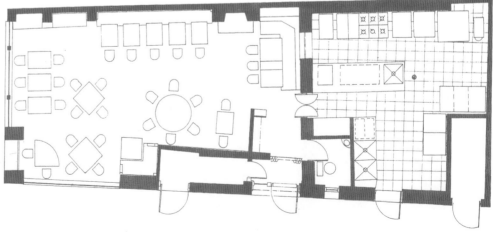

Architecture/Interior Design:
L. Bogdanow & Associates, Architects
Design Team:
Larry Bogdanow, Warren Ashworth, Dan Kohs, Paula Auhmada and Peter Codella
Graphic Design:
Julie Salestrom, Salestrom & Zingg
Photography:
Daniel Eifert and Ross Muir
Type:
Mediterranean
Size:
1,100 square feet
Project Completed:
January, 1990
Budget:
$100,000

Splendido

San Francisco, CA

At Splendido the fundamental concept was to recreate the ambience of a provincial Mediterranean fishing village. The designers wanted to capture the sense of place that such a small community might possess after generations. They wanted the "added-on look" of dwellings that had been worked-on over the years. There are heavy rustic beams and the entire restaurant is clad with real stacked rock walls. But the designers were looking for more than a recreation of the past. Their answer was to develop a system of illuminated sculptures that would become a bridge over time, something that would "be a relic of the future from the past." The response came in the form of several different types of lighting representing the restaurant's various areas. The function of the largest of these fixtures was as a room divider, and the response was a freestanding glass lamp that appears like a ghostly apparition. They almost seem to be made of scavenged pieces of flotsam that were crudely fastened together. Sand was placed in the bottom to give the feeling of a relic that had been unearthed. The light coming through the glass initially had a greenish cast, not very complementary on people's skin. To rectify this situation, the lighting designer took a piece of copper cloth and put it around the bulb. Now the bottom of the lamp has a pink color that reflects soft skin tones. The upper part of the light fades into a watery green color, a reference to the Mediterranean Sea. The pink light makes this green seem even more green.

So many sconces today appear to be half of something, so the lighting designer wanted to create a fixture for the dining room that would seem more complete. The solution was a glass piece held away from the wall by a pair of hands as if it were an offering. This is meant as a reference to a gift or the bestowal of something being handed down, and alludes back to the restaurant's notion of inheritance. The lighting designer cast a model of her own hands and since the desire was for the warm flame-like quality of glowing embers, the glass was given a torch-like appearance.

Eight columns break up a window wall overlooking the San Francisco Bay; another type of wall sconce was created to adorn them. Yearning to create a sense of interplay with the outside world, the desire was to capture a sense of movement. These fixtures were devised to appear as though they were serpents returning to the sea. They hold above them an irregular-shaped, circular piece of glass. Ringed in concentric circles, the glass has the look of water after a pebble has been thrown in. The lighting designer added sand to the center to diffuse the light. The bar area at Splendido caters to a faster paced crowd so it has a much more modern feeling. The light fixtures correspond to this contemporary look by appearing like heralding trumpets. The designer deliberately broke with tradition by not having them shine up the column. The glass is colorless and a little lid on the top holds the bulb and contains the light, creating a sense of energy.

Architecture/Interior Design:
Kuleto Consulting & Design
Design Team:
Charles Thompson, Pat Kuleto and Pam Morris
Graphic Design:
Kathleen McMullen
Photography:
Dennis Anderson
Type:
Pan Mediterranean
Size:
7,200 square feet
Project Completed:
November, 1990
Budget:
$2,200,000

St. Paul Grill
St. Paul, MN

The St. Paul Grill is meant to be a reinterpretation of the quintessential American Grill. The designers wanted to express this by creating an architectural space of timelessness and permanence. They wanted the restaurant to somehow reinforce the tradition that St. Paul is the city where the East ends and Minneapolis the city where the West begins.

Part of the architectural challenge involved creating an addition which would be integrated with the existing hotel built in 1910. Yet the restaurant had to create its own identity in order to stand on its own. The solution presents a bright and lively image from Rice Park across the street. Interior spaces were designed to take advantage of the park's unique urban views. The resulting spaces are a sequence of animated, light-filled rooms with an aura of comfort appropriate for a traditional American grill.

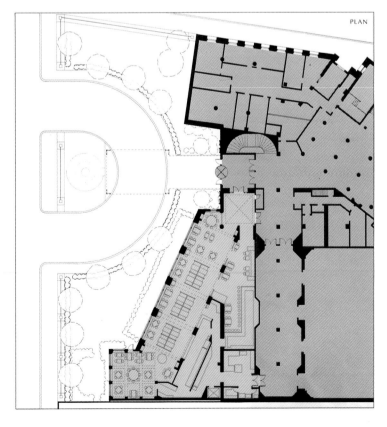

PLAN

Architectutre/Interior Design:
Hammel Green and Abrahamson, Inc.
Design Team:
**Daniel Avchen, Gary Reetz, Thomas Whitcomb, David Howd,
Joan Soranno and Mark Ludgatis**
Graphic Design:
McKracken Brooks Communications and Foote Marketing Group
Photography:
Tim Street-Porter
Type:
American Grill
Size:
8,000 square feet
Project Completed:
October, 1990
Budget:
$1,800,000

Surf 'n Turf

Matsuyama-shi, Japan

The client, the owner of a chain of restaurants in Japan, wanted to create something different. His desire was to devise an establishment that would be uniquely American in style. The designer initially met with the restaurateur over dinner, where, while surveying the menu, he noticed a listing for "surf 'n turf." It was an American expression he had not yet heard and one he found quite humorous. With that, the idea for the restaurant was born. From that initial response to a bit of American slang, the designer created a restaurant of great whimsy and caprice. A system of furniture and fixtures was fabricated that actually caricature the restaurant's own fare. In doing so, a fanciful world was created; one hopelessly lost in an imaginary, cartoon-like fantasy.

Indeed, the designer found much of his inspiration for Surf 'n Turf in Japanese "B" movies, in America's slang and its hip gestures, and, of course, in comic strips. "I wanted people to know what it would feel like to be a part of animation," the designer said. In Japan, people traditionally greet each other with a bow. So it seemed only appropriate that this American restaurant's front door should greet customers with a good ol' American handshake. The door handle was designed to resemble a cartoon hand. Fabricated from bronze and in true cartoon fashion, it has four digits instead of five. The push plate on the other side is a similar hand reaching up to give the patrons a "high four" as they exit.

The designer noticed that, "the Japanese love to eat sea urchin," so he designed chandeliers for the entry area that would resemble these creatures. Also included was a large circular mosaic in the center of the floor that repeats many of the restaurant's motifs. All of the restaurant's cabinetry was constructed in Japan. The *ushi* coat closet takes its inspiration from a cow or a bull and comes complete with a set of horns made of sculpted wood. Its two door pulls were fabricated to resemble a bull's nose complete with a ring through it and a cow's tail. A small display cabinet with glass horns was created to appear animated, as though it has stepped from the silver screen and begun to dance.

The restaurant is slightly lower than the entry level, so a railing was created to help customers maneuver the steps. The newel posts are figures with puffed-up chests and thin tapering legs. These were designed to appear as though they are bowing to patrons as they enter the restaurant. The designer has begun to set the tone for a restaurant that is a unique blend of American and Japanese cultures.

He had the vestibule podium, with its distended beer belly, cast in bronze. Like all the fixtures in the restaurant, it serves a comedic purpose as well as a functional one. The columns were constructed of ferro concrete and painted with yellow polka dots.

Lighting in the dining room comes in many different representational forms. Finding further inspiration in the food the restaurant serves, the designer created lighting to resemble sea anemones and sea cucumbers, while the chandeliers are constructed replete with squid legs. All of these pieces are made of copper and hand-blown glass. The tables are made of sculpted wood with metal bases, and the paw-like chairs have sculpted wooden feet painted bright yellow. All the restaurant's tables, chairs and banquettes were constructed in Chicago and shipped to Japan. For the bar area, "the muscle beach railing," a line of bicep flexing cacti, was installed to cordon off the space. Another dancing display cabinet, this time with bronze feet, perches behind the bar. But perhaps the designer's *piece de resistance* is a Godzilla wall sconce that actually appears to be breathing fire. At Surf 'n Turf the designer put Japanese and American culture on a collision course. The resulting explosion is a brilliant and whimsical hallucination.

Architecture/Interior Design:
Jordan Mozer & Associates, Ltd.
Design Team:
Jordan Mozer, Principal
John Bolchert, Michael Suomi, Larry Traxler
Graphic Design:
Jordan Mozer
Photography:
Takeichi Photo
Type:
American
Size:
5,500 square feet
Project Completed:
January, 1992
Budget:
$900,000

Tatou

New York, NY

Tatou is unique in that it is a supper club complete with a stage and nightly performances by a blues band. However, as the evening wears on it reinvents itself. Tables and chairs are removed from the center of the dining room and stacked away, creating a dance floor for a kinetic disco. So it is no surprise that the dining room comes complete with synchronized lighting. The spatial arrangement is centrally oriented to the stage while the bar acts as an anteroom for the main entrance. Upstairs there is a quieter private club. The concept has been a huge success in New York and the operators are planning on expanding to new locations in Los Angeles and Miami.

The designers worked closely with the owners from the beginning and were instrumental in developing all the various facets that make Tatou distinctive. The restaurant has a warm, comfortable "lived-in" look, that is reminiscent of a southern opera house or old vaudevillian theater. Antique mirrors flank the raised platforms to the right and left of the main dining area. Satyr-headed newel posts line the parapet wall to reinforce the restaurant's already theatrical setting. These gilded, bust-topped pilasters are actually lamps and carry a shade over their heads. They are used for direct lighting at tables, as well as auxiliary lighting throughout the room. These unusual lamps are combined with traditional pendant style chandeliers, wall sconces, recessed fixtures and an illuminated coved ceiling to provide a full array of lighting sources and styles.

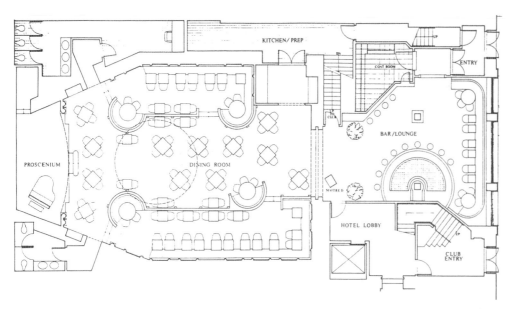

Architecture/Interior Design:
Haverson/Rockwell Architects
Design Team:
David Rockwell, Jay Haverson, David Pearson and R. Wade Johnson
Photography:
Paul Warchol
Type:
Nouvelle Southern American
Size:
8,000 square feet
Project Completed:
August, 1990
Budget:
$1,000,000

192

Tiger Restaurant

Lahaina, HI

This project involved the conversion of an existing bar and dining space that could best be described as "dingy and unappetizing." The restaurant had simply lost its luster. A vestige of the late sixties, this spot was a popular gathering place in the historic Lahaina area. Its clientele had changed with the times.

The new owners wished to re-establish a presence with specific physical requirements, but less specific architectural goals. The physical requirements presented a technical challenge for the architects. The new management wanted to employ the Oriental tradition of cooking at the table on a gas grill. But, this necessitated tabletop venting systems and required that the dining layout accommodate a system of under-floor ducts. With minimal clearances and demands for health and safety, this presented some problems.

The use of cooking tables related to some of the less specific architectural goals alluded to by the restaurant's owner. He wanted an open and airy sensation, one in which the lighting would be expressive and strategically placed. The intention was to create a fine dining establishment, so it was appropriate to have a sophisticated look. It also needed to allow for a broader accommodation of guests.

The resulting design solution evolved over a series of discussions with the owner. As issues arose, the architect's design ideas were presented to the owner and then modified to seek the proper balance. As a result of this careful dialogue between architect and client, the Tiger Restaurant is a unique blending of east and west—traditional and contemporary. The architect does not see this as a compromise, but rather views this balance of ideas and cultures as a reference to the cosmopolitan nature of Hawaii itself, a combination that is derived from the best of two worlds.

By utilizing eastern concepts of scale and symmetry, along with traditional materials like wood and stone and juxtaposing these with western objects in metal and glass, a striking balance was created. It is a balance that is neither traditional Japanese tea house nor slick American cafe. Rather, it is an entity born of two worlds to express a simple new vision.

TIGER
RESTAURANT

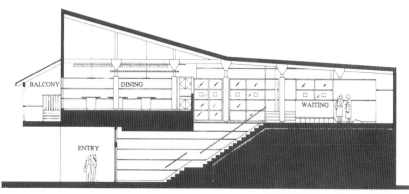

BALCONY

DINING

WAITING

ENTRY

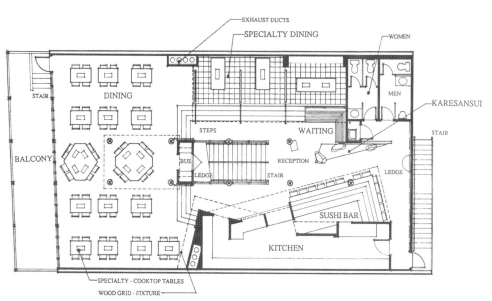

EXHAUST DUCTS

SPECIALTY DINING

WOMEN

STAIR

DINING

MEN

KARESANSUI

BALCONY

STEPS

WAITING

STAIR

BUS

LEDGE

RECEPTION

STAIR

LEDGE

SUSHI BAR

KITCHEN

SPECIALTY - COOKTOP TABLES

WOOD GRID - FIXTURE

Architecture/Interior Design:
AM Partners, Inc.
Design Team:
Charles Lau, AIA and Duane Hamada, AIA
Photography:
John DeMello, Franzen Photography
Type:
Korean Teppanyaki Cuisine
Size:
2,020 square feet
Project Completed:
February, 1989
Budget:
$1,200,000

Tropica

New York, NY

At Tropica, the designer wanted to recreate, "a beautiful tropical feeling without the typical cliches of a Caribbean restaurant." He set out to capture the look and seriousness of British colonial rule and combine it with the wit and whimsy of local architecture and native color.

Located in the former Pan Am Building, the restaurant was meant to be a restful oasis in midtown Manhattan. The low ceiling in the main dining room was given a greater sense of height with the insertion of a lattice framework. This gives the space the sensation of being inside an airy, tropical villa. The designer hid the lighting fixtures in this "roofline." He then outfitted them with dimmers so that they could be set to correspond with the time of day, creating an illusion. Light was also directed through small grilled panels, thus giving the effect of filtered sun. The dramatic illumination of specific objects creates a warm and sophisticated mood as well.

Gentle arches overhead separate one dining room from the next, and highlight the seemingly domestic scale of the space. The large open kitchen is gaily decorated with hand-painted tiles and also adds a homey touch to the dining area. Upholstered cane chairs and simple wooden tables underscore the informally elegant tone, while brass and frosted glass pendants and sconces are a hint at the urbane. Simple floral arrangements and discreetly placed carvings and artwork, typical of the Bahamas, foster the tropical ambience.

The adjacent bar exudes an old-fashioned, English Colonial atmosphere. A mural depicting a sandy beach backed by ultramarine waters enhances one wall, while the ceiling was painted to resemble a tropical sky.

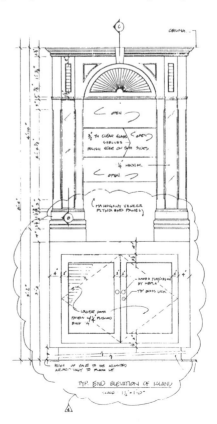

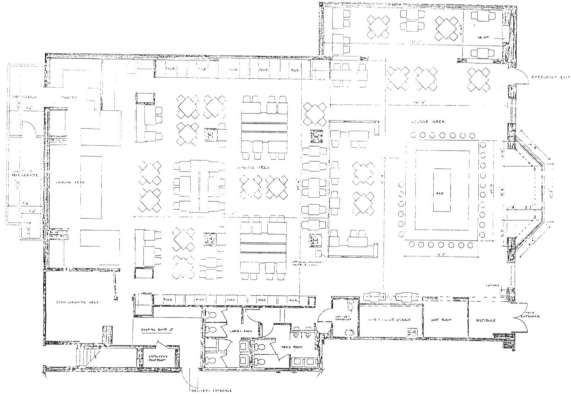

Architecture/Interior Design:
Frederick Brush Design Associates
Design Team:
Frederick Brush, Ben Chanhom and Kevin Ligos
Graphic Design:
Alexander Design
Photography:
Reyndell Stockman
Type:
Seafood
Size:
6,250 square feet
Project Completed:
May, 1990
Budget:
$1,900,000

Tutto Mare

La Jolla, CA

he Tutto Mare design concept loosely responds to the cylindrical form of the building itself. A combination of intersecting planes, curves, custom lighting, furnishings and colors was employed to emphasize functional relationships and movement. "One never arrives into an ideal space or dining area," the designer says. "Rather, one is led from one open area to another, being vaguely aware of the free motion of the sea." Indeed, it is the sea that provided the focus and inspiration for this large, glass-walled restaurant. The architect played with the use of light and angle to create smooth transitions between the various spaces. Curving, up-lit soffits utilize low watt halogen lighting. The soffits follow the bend of the walls and assist in giving the spaces a soft free flowing quality.

The clean lined reception area with its sleek, futuristic styling has an elegant and understated look vaguely reminiscent of the '60s. The terrazzo floors are a custom pattern of selected color mixes. The shelf behind the reception desk, a metaphor for an anchor or a fishing hook, projects through a slit-like wall opening. The space creates a mood-setting style and an appropriate welcome for the adjoining bar and dining rooms. The curving main bar is topped with granite. The distressed wrought iron finished stools are upholstered in water buffalo hide that was imported from the Philippines. Glass shelves behind the bar hold liquor bottles and are back-lit using fiber optic strips. The two shelves run the bar's entire 30-foot length. A silicone adhesive was used to hold the fiber optic strips to the back of the glass shelves and in as much are invisible to the eye. The lights can be continually rotated for a spectrum of colors or remain in one particular range or hue. The light gives the liquor bottles a special glow. The designer prefers a luminous turquoise because he feels this falls within Tutto Mare's palate. The objective was to shift patrons' attention away from the more formal waiting area and into the restaurant itself.

Adjoining the bar is the granite topped cable lit food display counter, its soffit decorated with a relief showing a school of fish. Here there are a series of gaily upholstered banquettes. Completely movable, they were built on standard stainless steel equipment legs. This area continues the architect's philosophy of spatial progression by creating a transitional buffer between the food preparation areas and the dining rooms beyond. The floors in the upper dining area were carpeted. All wood is French or domestic ash and all wall bases are stainless steel. In the bathrooms, the vanity countertops were constructed of sandblasted glass lit from below by linear incandescent lamps.

Utilizing colors in a range between yellow, orange, raw umber and ochre as well as gray and turquoise, the designer was able to coordinate a program that captures the essence of the sea. The design scheme enhances the overall look of the restaurant by coordinating color, with furniture and fixtures, as well as fabrics.

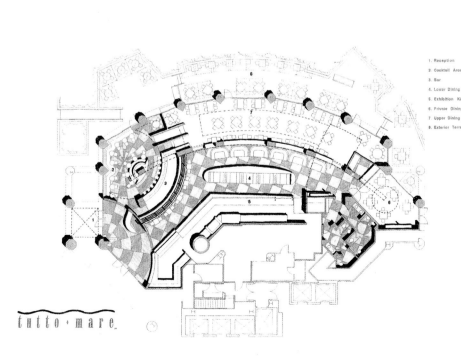

1. Reception
2. Cocktail Area
3. Bar
4. Lower Dining Area
5. Exhibition Kitchen
6. Private Dining
7. Upper Dining
8. Exterior Terrace Dining

tutto·mare

Bar Area

View toward Private Dining

Reception Area

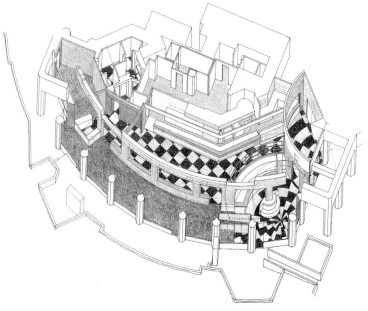

Architecture/Interior Design:
James Gillam Architects
Design Team:
James Gillam
Graphic Design:
Primo Angeli
Photography:
Anne Garrison and David Hewitt
Type:
Italian Seafood
Size:
8,200 square feet
Project Completed:
November, 1991

Undici

San Francisco, CA

*L*ocated on 11th Street in San Francisco's SOMA District, Undici means eleven in Italian. Built in a former warehouse, it was transformed from raw industrial space with high ceilings, into the welcoming courtyard of an ancient Italian villa. The result is a Mediterranean-inspired dining room that has atmosphere without sacrificing comfort. It seems only appropriate that such a restaurant would feature hearty, country-style Sicilian cooking.

The designer employed the use of faux paints and finishes to capture the look of age. The room was painted in warm earth tones and features a trompe l'oeil grape cluster pattern on the walls. The floor has the look of worn and weathered stone. The designer enhanced the look of the room by utilizing faux-style classical paintings and sculptures created by a local artist as well as a small quiet fountain. Custom wrought-iron grillwork and vine covered chandeliers also add a touch of old Sicily. To complete the decor and add to the restaurant's courtyard atmosphere, the designer hung banners from the rafters that were painted with Italian country motifs.

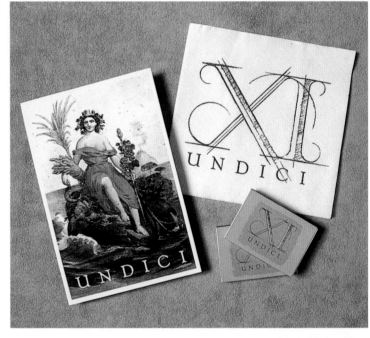

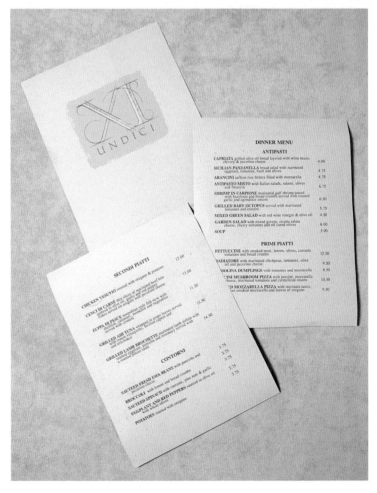

Architecture/Interior Design:
Tim Dale
Design Team:
Tim Dale and Art of the Muse
Graphic Design:
Tim Dale and Jain Hagerstone
Photography:
Judy Reed
Type:
Southern Italian
Size:
3,000 square feet
Project Completed:
April, 1990
Budget:
$150,000

Vivere

Chicago, IL

The name Vivere, means "to live" and this dining room, located in The Italian Village complex of restaurants, has adopted the spiral as a symbol of persistence and abiding love. The spiral is a common motif in baroque architecture and one that is generously repeated throughout the bar and dining room. Vivere is the initial venture by the grand-children of the restaurant's founder. Located in Chicago's Loop for the last 60 years, the redux for this dining room was meant to establish a sanctuary from the city's hard-edged financial district.

Vivere's custom design—just about everything was handmade—was carried out by more than 60 small manu-facturers and artists. But the designer claims it cost the same as the "direct from the catalog" interior he was hired to do for a Chicago Pizza Chain. He refers to the restaurant's style as, "idiosyncratic post-industrial Italian baroque." He found his inspiration in Italian architecture, but claims his real ob-jective was to fuse ancient with modern. The door to the entryway establishes the tempo. The handle is a finely crafted cast bronze scroll that was cleverly bolted into place. The door's copper kickplate playfully unwinds itself from the ma-hogany door. Copper rivets give the bar an antique look and its granite top ends in a swirl of contrasting stone. The bar-stools, with their wiry frames, are covered in soft gray velvet. Even the dining room's color palette of terra cotta, burnt or-ange, green and black found its inspiration in the "old world." An illuminated cornice was decorated with sand-blasted industrial glass that was leaded into frames painted to look like gold-leaf. But the inspiration is purely tongue-in-cheek, with silk draperies supported by iron shackles that are traditionally used for aircraft carriers. Spirals had been a mo-tif present in the old restaurant as well. And the designer transformed the spiral theme into a parody of itself; there are spirals everywhere. Thirteen foot copper spirals swirl down from the ceiling and plaster walls seem to be curling down from overhead. Even the chair and booth backs end in spi-rals. The unusual central chandelier, with its inlaid leaded glass spiral, had its origins as the nose cone of an airplane.

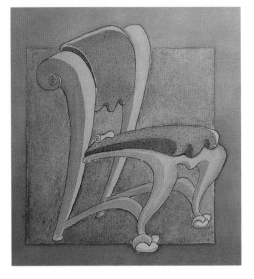

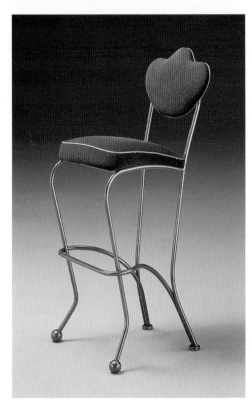

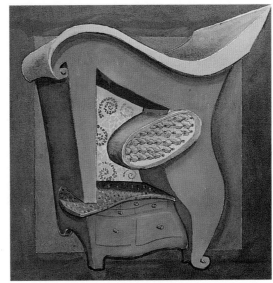

Architecture/Interior Design:
Jordan Mozer & Associates Ltd.
Design Team:
Jordan Mozer
Graphic Design:
Jordan Mozer & Associates Ltd.
Photography:
David Clifton
Type:
Italian
Size:
5,500 square feet
Project Completed:
September, 1990
Budget:
$1,000,000

Vivo

Chicago, IL

Located on West Randolph Street in Chicago's wholesale produce market, Vivo is slightly "off-the-beaten-track." The surrounding area is a stark panorama of water towers, meat packing plants and old warehouses. The restaurant is at the center of this rather run-down, but historic neighborhood that has served as Chicago's fruit and vegetable market for generations. Indeed, its seedy location has actually been part of the restaurant's draw and has the benefit of allowing the chef to hand pick all the ingredients.

Outside, an illuminated awning serves as an outdoor cafe. Heavy curtains at the front door act as an effective weather barrier. The raw, sand-blasted brick walls were embellished with several thousand stacked wine bottles. The ceiling joists and ducts were painted black. The sixteen-foot-high space was then dramatically lit by 150 long-beam pin spots that bathe tables in streams of light for a softening effect.

The rough hewn Italian granite bar runs nearly the entire length of the room. The unique tables, chairs and barstools are hand fabricated metal that had been upholstered in multi-colored leather. Vivo has 80 table seats, ten barstools and a downstairs lounge that accommodates 50. This lower level serves as a guest waiting area as well as a romantic after-dinner rendezvous. A twisting metal staircase leads to the vertical shaft that formerly housed the building's freight elevator. This is Vivo's most requested perch. It now provides space for a small alcove with a single table for eight and affords a unique view of the dining room. An open kitchen lends to the restaurant's theatrical quality and allows guests to watch food preparation.

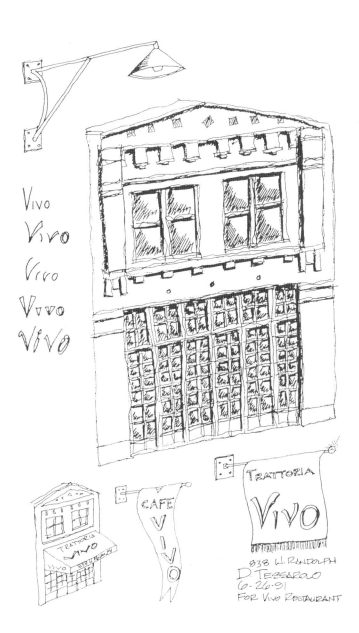

Vivo
Vivo
Vivo
Vivo
Vivo

TRATTORIA
VIVO

838 W. RANDOLPH
D. TESSAROLO
6·26·91
FOR VIVO RESTAURANT

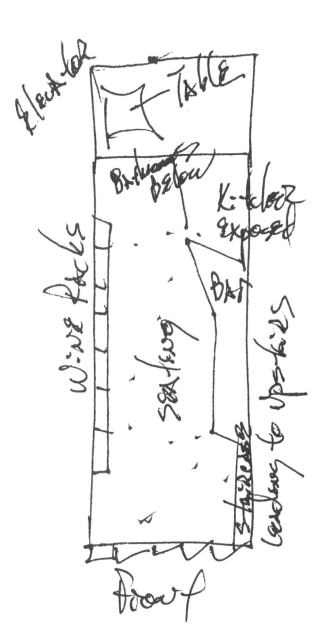

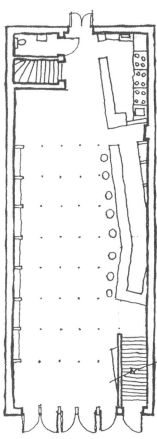

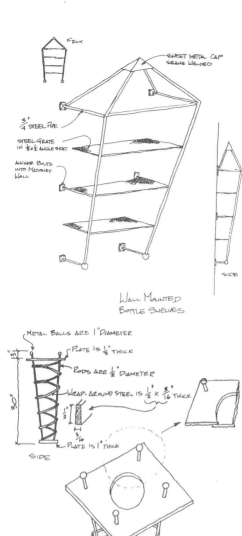

FRONT

SHEET METAL CAP
SEAMS WELDED

3/4" STEEL PIPE

STEEL GRATE
IN 4x4 ANGLE SEAT

ANCHOR BOLTS
INTO MASONRY
WALL

SIDE

WALL MOUNTED
BOTTLE SHELVES

METAL BALLS ARE 1" DIAMETER

PLATE IS 1/2" THICK

RODS ARE 1/2" DIAMETER

WRAP AROUND STEEL IS 1/2" X 3/16" THICK

PLATE IS 1" THICK

SIDE

VIVO
WINE BUCKET
STAND

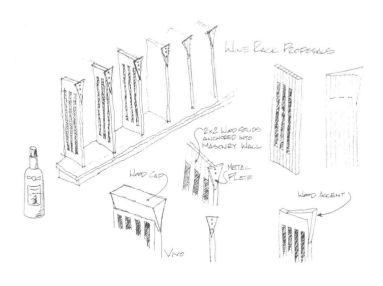

WINE RACK PROPOSALS

2x2 WOOD STUDS
ANCHORED INTO
MASONRY WALL

WOOD CAP

METAL
PLATE

WOOD ACCENT

VIVO

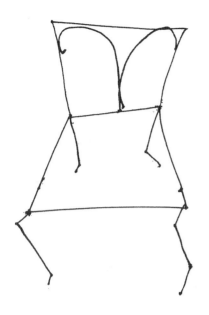

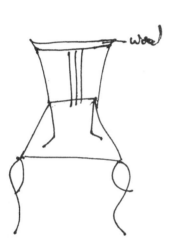

wood

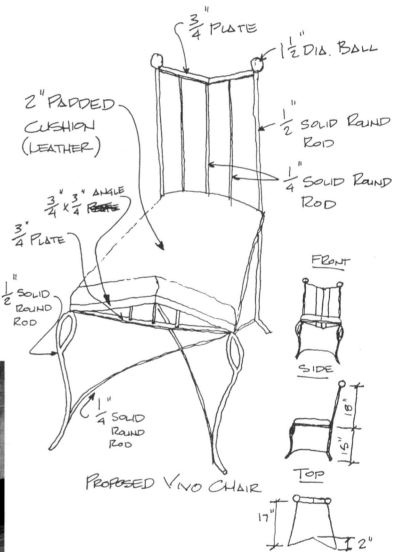

3/4" PLATE

1 1/2" DIA. BALL

2" PADDED CUSHION (LEATHER)

1/2" SOLID ROUND ROD

1/4" SOLID ROUND ROD

3/4" x 3/4" ANGLE PLATE

3/4" PLATE

1/2" SOLID ROUND ROD

1/4" SOLID ROUND ROD

FRONT

SIDE

18"

15"

TOP

17"

2"

PROPOSED VINO CHAIR

Architecture/Interior Design:
Kleiner Design
Design Team:
Jerry Kleiner and Dan Tessarolo
Graphic Design:
Ellisa Knopper and Mark Anderson, Kleiner Design
Photography:
Mark Ballog and Steve Arazmus
Type:
Italian
Size:
4,500 square feet
Project Completed:
September, 1991
Budget:
$500,000

Water Grill

Los Angeles, CA

The Water Grill is meant to be *the* sophisticated Los Angeles supper club of the '90s. In a style the designer calls, "one step removed from art moderne," it is somewhat classical in its lines. Add to that a bit of Hollywood panache and you have a restaurant that redefines the ambience of a golden era in dining.

Upon entering the restaurant, guests pass into the club through a heavy swag of royal purple velvet. An entry ramp, paved in terrazzo, was done in a pattern of gracefully undulating curves. The waiting area, with its long sofa upholstered in green and blue leather, provides a welcoming place for guests to sit.

Fixtures of hand-blown, illuminated glass were used in the cocktail lounge area as were aniegre wood and zinc. Situated at the forefront of the restaurant, this space becomes a hub of activity. The lounge offers a subtle mood of formality with its wood paneled walls, wood flooring and splashes of gold and purple upholstery. The most prominent feature in the space is the oyster bar with its daily display of fresh seafood. Caricatures of oxygen bubbles that have seemingly risen from the depths of the ocean floor find their place painted on the ceiling. There is also a school of fanciful wire fish suspended over the bar.

Beyond the cocktail lounge is the dining room. It has been set apart from the rest of the space by streamlined ribbed glass windows and a curvilinear wall. It is a blending of what the designer determined to be the proper amount of exposure and intimacy. Adorned in heavily woven fabrics and carpet in tones of teal and gold, its high paneled booths offer privacy without closing the space off. The walls have black and silver molding recessed in the aniegere panels and set in an oblique pattern. Limestone blocks in shades of gold and ocher lend a sense of strength and timelessness. The designers intent was to draw architectural elements inward for all to see. The dining room ceiling, painted in gradations of purple and teal, creates a background for the suspended luminous glass fixtures. The vibrant wall murals are the single most important unifying force within the restaurant, whimsically depicting a combination of caricatures of famous Los Angeles landmarks, set amongst a background of the sea. Toward the rear of the space, the open kitchen, provides a rich source of entertainment and color for the patrons' enjoyment. Sophisticated in its design and ambience, the Water Grill evokes an air of relaxed formality.

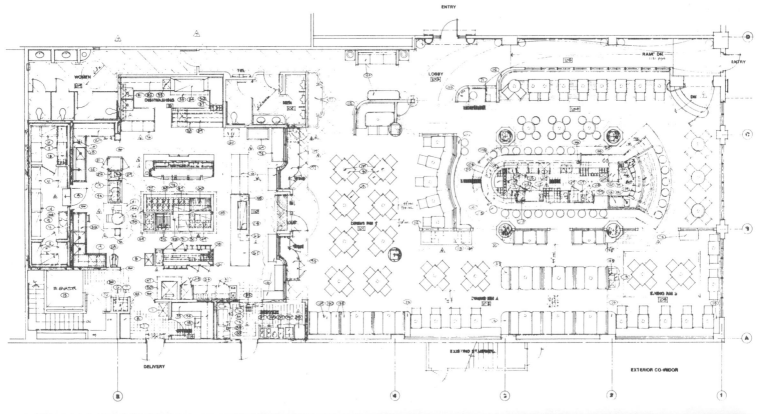

Architecture/Interior Design:
Hatch Design Group
Design Team:
Jeff Hatch, Sam Hatch and Jackie Hanson
Photography:
Martin Fine
Type:
Seafood
Size:
7,950 square feet
Project Completed:
June, 1991
Budget:
$1,700,000

West Broadway

New York, NY

est Broadway, a street level bistro spread across two adjoining buildings in New York's Soho neighborhood, required only minor renovation. Because of budgetary restrictions there were no major alterations in the structure itself. Formerly a Mexican restaurant, it was primarily in need of a fresh coat of paint and redecorating. It was the desire of the client, a dealer in twentieth century decorative arts, to furnish the restaurant with pieces from his collection of French and American lighting and furniture from the 1950s.

The construction and redecoration involved stripping the space down to bare bones and then applying new surfaces. The designer's strategy was to make a refined and inviting setting for the vintage objects. He accomplished this by his inventive use of ordinary materials. A long wall that runs parallel to the bar area was outfitted with banquet seating upholstered in alternating gold and black vinyl. The wall above was painted in a harlequin pattern in the same colors. The dining area is split between two separate levels, each a half flight above or below the bar area. The chandeliers, designed by Serge Mouille, were combined with wall murals originally commissioned for the Roseland Ballroom in New York. The remaining raw elements were painted black to appear recessive and create a graphic contrast to the vivid patterns and textures used in the design program. The firm received a citation in the American Institute of Architects—N.Y.C. 1992 Design Awards Program for their work on West Broadway.

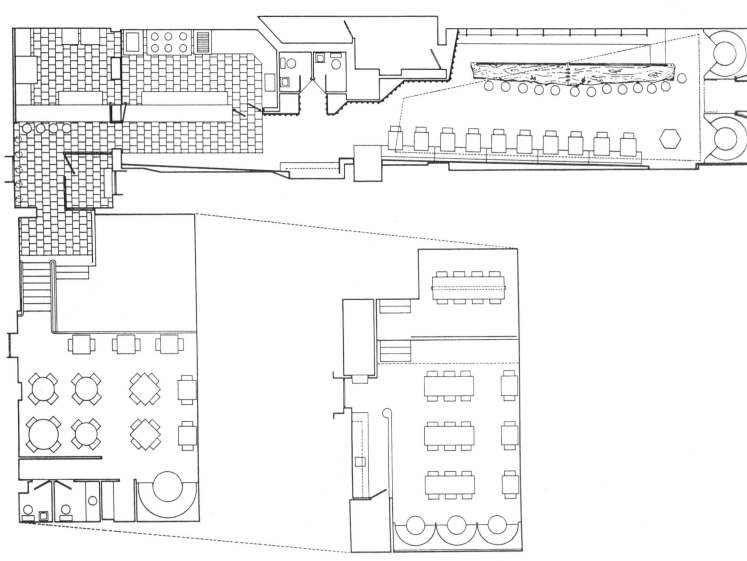

© 1991 Peter Mauss/ESTO

Architecture/Interior Design:
Henry I. Myerberg Architects
Design Team:
Henry I. Myerberg, Principal in Charge
Ann O'Dell and Toby O'Rorke
Photography:
Peter Mauss/ESTO
Type:
Bistro
Size:
4,000 square feet
Project Completed:
September, 1991

Zen Palate

New York, NY

This gourmet vegetarian food shop and bistro in midtown Manhattan has the Far East appeal of an old world oriental restaurant combined with today's cutting edge style. Designed as an interpretation of an Asian cafe in Paris, Zen Palate occupies the ground floor of two brownstone buildings. Three sets of double doors at the front allow an eating bar to be opened up to a small sidewalk cafe. In Manhattan, where space is at a premium, this extra seating can be utilized during pleasant weather. Inside, the bar serves patrons eating alone or those in a hurry. For those dining at a more relaxed pace, the restaurant offers three separate dining spaces that are reached from an entrance off an adjoining side street.

Centered around a U-shaped plan, the restaurant maximizes seating capacity by isolating cooking and other service functions at the core, and to one side of the space. In this way, the kitchen remains at the center of two separate and very distinct food operations, each with their own menu. At the back of the restaurant a former garden area was enclosed to create a bar. A skylight was added to bring in light and create a feeling of openness. Seating in this cheerful daytime space is provided by traditional French bistro chairs.

Spanish terra cotta tiles imported from Barcelona were used as floor covering. Functional as well as practical, they create a sense of continuity and serve to unify the space while giving the restaurant an "earthy" quality. The walls were given a special finish to simulate the color and texture of a pumpkin and imbue the dining areas with a warm patina. Up-lit cable lights and cone shaped parchment paper sconces make the most of the painted surfaces by reflecting light to create a soft glow. The bar, paneled walls, trim and all doors are made of a stained Honduran mahogany that adds to this bistro's subdued elegance. Decorative touches were kept simple and to a minimum. They include a large statue of Buddha and a model of a Buddhist temple that occupies an unusual pedestal.

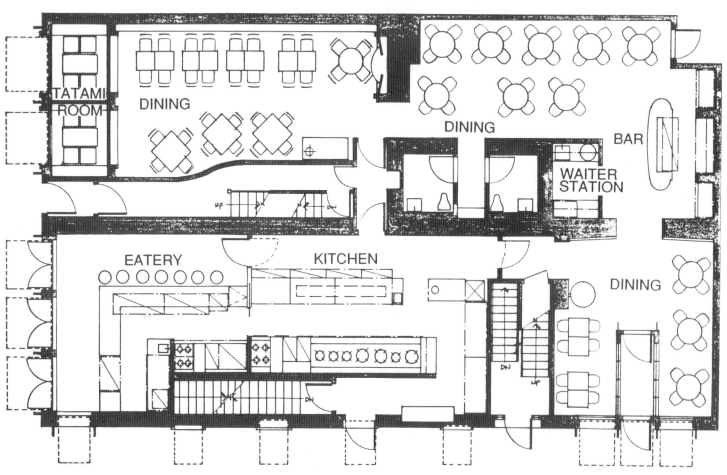

Architecture/Interior Design:
Tony Chi & Associates
Design Team:
Tony Chi, Albert Chen
Graphic Design:
Bill Kobasz
Photography:
Dub Rogers
Type:
Vegetarian
Size:
3,500 square feet
Project Completed:
September, 1991
Budget:
$450,000

Appendix

Allied Architects
118 Hawthorne Street
San Francisco, CA 94107
(415) 495-2445

AM Partners, Inc.
1164 Bishop Street, Suite 1000
Honolulu, HI 96813
(808) 526-2828

Ann Sheehan-Lipton Interiors
6355 Waterman Boulevard
St. Louis, MO 63108
(314) 725-6409

Aumiller Youngquist, P.C.
111 E. Busse Avenue #603
Mt. Prospect, IL 60056
(708) 253-3761

Barry Design Associates
11601 Wilshire Boulevard, Suite 102
Los Angeles, CA 90025
(310) 478-6081

Bethe Cohen Design Associates
150 E. Campbell Avenue #102
Campbell, CA 95008
(408) 379-4051

Brantner Design Associates
633 North Almont Drive
Los Angeles, CA 90069
(310) 247-1090

Brock Simini, Architects
614 East Capitol Street
Washington, DC 20003
(202) 543-7058

D'Amico + Partners, Inc.
1402 First Avenue South
Minneapolis, MN 55403
(612) 334-3366

Tim Dale
374 11th Street
San Francisco, CA 94103
(415) 431-3337

Darrell Hawthorne Architecture
1014 Noe Street
San Francisco, CA 94114
(415) 282-2955

David Kellen Architects
2936 Nebraska Avenue
Santa Monica, CA 90404
(310) 453-1615

Design Solutions
P.O. Box 460817
San Francisco, CA 94146
(415) 255-8186

Dorf Associates Interior Design Inc.
106 East 19th Street
New York, NY 10003
(212) 473-9667

Engstrom Design Group, Inc.
5725 Paradise Drive #380
Corte Madera, CA 94925
(415) 924-0560

Frederick Brush Design Associates
53 East Avenue
Norwalk, CT 06851
(203) 846-0828

Guthrie Friedlander Architects
575 Francisco Street
San Francisco, CA 94133
(415) 771-9991

Hammel Green and Abrahamson, Inc.
1201 Harmon Place
Minneapolis, MN 55403
(612) 332-3944

Hatch Design Group
3198D Airport Loop Drive
Costa Mesa, CA 92626
(714) 979-8385

Haverson/Rockwell Architects, P.C.
18 West 27th Street
New York, NY 10001
(212) 889-4182

Henry I. Myerberg Architects
6 West 18th Street
New York, NY 10011
(212) 924-7222

Interim Office of Architecture
10 Heron Street
San Francisco, CA 94103
(415) 864-7226

James Gillam Architects
1841 Powell Street
San Francisco, CA 94133
(415) 378-1120

Jordan Mozer & Associates, Ltd
228 W. Illinois
Chicago, IL 60610
(312) 661-0060

Kleiner Design
560 Fulton Street
Chicago, IL 60606
(312) 831-0400

Kotas/Pantaleoni
70 Zoe Street
San Francisco, CA 94107
(415) 495-4051

Kuleto Consulting & Design
Foot of Spring Street
Sausalito, CA 94965
(415) 331-0880

L. Bogdanow & Associates, Architects
75 Spring Street
New York, NY 10012
(212) 966-0313

Marve Cooper Design
2120 W. Grand Avenue
Chicago, IL 60612
(312) 733-4250

Mesher Shing & Associates
3300 Smith Tower
Seattle, WA 98104
(206) 622-4981

Muzingo Associates
2288 Westwood Boulevard, Suite 210
Los Angeles, CA 90064
(310) 470-9181

O'Brien & Associates Design, Inc.
222 Washington Avenue #12
Santa Monica, CA 90403
(310) 458-9177

Paul Draper & Associates
4106 Swiss Avenue
Dallas, TX 75204
(214) 824-8352

Pentagram Architectural Services, P.C.
212 Fifth Avenue
New York, NY 10010
(212) 683-7071

Ron Meyers Design
7711 Fountain Avenue
Los Angeles, CA 90046
(213) 851-7576

Sayles Graphic Design
308 Eighth Street
Des Moines, IA 50309
(515) 243-2922

Shawn E. Hall Designs
235 Greenwich #F
San Francisco, CA 94133
(415) 986-3518

Sprinkle Robey Architects
454 Soledad
San Antonio, TX 78205
(512) 227-7722

Steve Bowles Designs
2712 January
St. Louis, MO 63139
(314) 644-4886

Studio Arquitectura
101 West Marcy Street
Santa Fe, NM 87501
(505) 982-5338

Tainer Associates Ltd.
213 West Institute Place, Suite 301
Chicago, IL 60610
(312) 951-1656

To Design
152 Corte Anita
Greenbrae, CA 94904
(415) 461-6705

Tony Chi & Associates
215 Park Avenue South, Suite 702
New York, NY 10003
(212) 353-8860

Turett Collaborative Architects
45 West 18th Street 7th floor
New York, NY 10011
(212) 627-2530

Index

Design Team

Acknowledgments

Producing this project involved the collaboration of many talented people. As I worked toward making this book a reality, I found that it was really the contributors who expressed their visions in their restaurant designs that make this book special. I share my appreciation and thank you to all of the people involved who contributed their time, support, and ideas.

Thank you to Christian Simon, from San Jose State University, who worked a summer internship with me on this project.

Thank you to the several restaurant designers who shared their point of view in the written essays. They are Shawn Hall, David Kellen and Larry Bogdanow.

Thank you to all the visionary restaurateurs who conceived the variety of dining concepts presented here. It is the designers, architects, and photographers—and their spectacular work—that really make this book possible.

Most of all, I would like to thank the staff at PBC International—especially Kevin Clark, managing editor; Susan Kapsis, project editor; Richard Liu, creative director, Carrie Abel, art director, Anthony Trama, book designer, and Joanne Caggiano. I am also indebted to former editor, Chet Dallas. The hard work and dedication put forth on this project is greatly appreciated.

Judi Radice
San Francisco